Dealing with Staff Turnover

Dealing with Staff Turnover

Systems that Make Schools More Resilient in Times of Change

Elizabeth Dampf

ROWMAN & LITTLEFIELD
Lanham • Boulder • New York • London

Published by Rowman & Littlefield
An imprint of The Rowman & Littlefield Publishing Group, Inc.
4501 Forbes Boulevard, Suite 200, Lanham, Maryland 20706
www.rowman.com

86-90 Paul Street, London EC2A 4NE, United Kingdom

Copyright © 2024 by Elizabeth Dampf

All rights reserved. No part of this book may be reproduced in any form or by any electronic or mechanical means, including information storage and retrieval systems, without written permission from the publisher, except by a reviewer who may quote passages in a review.

British Library Cataloguing in Publication Information Available

Library of Congress Cataloging-in-Publication Data

Names: Dampf, Elizabeth, 1985– author.
Title: Dealing with staff turnover : systems that make schools more resilient in times of change / Elizabeth Dampf.
Description: Lanham, Maryland : Rowman & Littlefield, 2024. | Includes bibliographical references. | Summary: "Dealing With Staff Turnover: Systems that Make Schools More Resilient in Times of Change lays out a process for organizing, publishing, and promoting systems. It explains how to frame and embed them into teachers' practice"—Provided by publisher.
Identifiers: LCCN 2023055890 (print) | LCCN 2023055891 (ebook) | ISBN 9781475874501 (cloth) | ISBN 9781475874518 (paperback) | ISBN 9781475874525 (epub)
Subjects: LCSH: Teacher turnover—United States. | School personnel management—United States. | School management and organization—United States.
Classification: LCC LB2833.2 .D36 2024 (print) | LCC LB2833.2 (ebook) | DDC 371.140973—dc23/eng/20231229
LC record available at https://lccn.loc.gov/2023055890
LC ebook record available at https://lccn.loc.gov/2023055891

Contents

Introduction: Stop Complaining, Start Confronting	vii
Step 1: Prioritize the Practical	1
Step 2: Establish and Calibrate	11
Step 3: Build Your Publication	27
Step 4: Train Your Leaders	37
Step 5: Onboard New Teachers	47
Step 6: Promote the Library to Current Staff	61
Step 7: Maintain, Expand, and Advertise	71
Conclusion	79
Bibliography	81
About the Author	83

Introduction

Stop Complaining, Start Confronting

HOW TO DEAL WITH TURNOVER, EVEN IF YOU CAN'T PREVENT IT

If only you were an emperor, you'd get us out of this mess in a jiffy. You'd pay teachers what they're worth and hire unlimited support staff. You'd strengthen the connections between teacher preparation programs and actual schools, so prospective educators would have more practice before taking charge of their own classrooms. You'd generate serious cultural respect for the profession, which has largely been dismissed as a cutesy hobby for warm-hearted saps. You, like most leaders, understand the big picture changes needed to attract, develop, and retain high-quality teachers.

But you're not an emperor. You're a school leader just trying to survive the tornado of turnover currently ransacking the industry. You don't have the power to make sweeping systemic changes. On the contrary, you sometimes feel like you don't have the power to impact much of anything, given the tense social, political, and economic quagmire we call American education.

That's why preventing turnover feels impossible—not challenging, not tedious, but truly *impossible*—for the everyday administrator. I'm not here to contradict that feeling. I don't have the perfect recipe to prevent turnover in your district, and, like you, I don't have the power to enact sweeping educational reform. I'm actually in the same boat as you are, trying to help teachers in my district feel supported and fulfilled so that they stick around. The fact is this: ordinary school leaders like us can't always prevent turnover. It's going to happen. That's not defeatism. It's reality.

This book is all about dealing with that reality. While we can't necessarily prevent turnover, we can definitely respond to it by funneling more resources—especially our time and attention—into effective induction. If you just rolled your eyes, hear me out: educator turnover will be painfully high for several more years, maybe even decades. We are dealing with teacher shortages from both sides of the pipeline: enrollment in teacher preparation programs has been on the decline since the 2010's, *and* veterans are leaving the profession at shockingly high rates.

On top of that, educators are leaving current positions for better ones faster and faster, now that the job market favors them. This isn't going away next year or the year after that or the year after that. If you intend to stay in educational leadership for a while, you are going to face turnover for the foreseeable future. You may as well have a plan for dealing with it. An ideal plan will do the following:

- Anticipate, prioritize, and meet incoming teachers' material needs by creating an organized environment
- Provide fast, clear, consistent answers to common procedural questions by connecting teachers to a library of on-demand information
- Free teachers to focus on instruction immediately by helping them learn basic procedures quickly

You may find this list practical to the point of being incomplete. Where is the focus on emotional support? On mentoring? On culture? Why does this list cling staunchly to the physical and procedural ins and outs?

It is because those are the things you can control the most fully. The other aspects of new teacher satisfaction are within your power to *influence* but not to *guarantee*. For example, you can establish a mentoring program, train mentors, and monitor their work, but you cannot guarantee that mentors will not go rogue, giving poor advice or insufficient support to their proteges. You cannot *force* them to give effective feedback, listen with compassion, or represent the school positively.

Mentors are people with their own needs, crises, and biases, so they might come up short sometimes, even for perfectly understandable reasons. It's simply not within your power to control every aspect of an interpersonal program like mentoring, which is why, as a leader, you would be foolish to assume your mentor program alone will reduce turnover.

Then there's culture. In these turbulent times, culture matters more than ever before, and I suggest exploring the wide array of literature explaining how leaders can impact team culture. A word of caution, though: as much as you can influence the culture of your building by setting high expectations and initiating warm collegialism among your staff, you cannot control how teachers feel, think, and act in any given moment, and a change in culture isn't the same thing as a stable staff.

In fact, many leaders discover, after putting in the time to change a building's culture, that they have actually triggered turnover. It's the good kind of turnover, the emigration of the lazy and cantankerous, but still, new people are flooding in, a bundle of needs on their back.

So, what can you control? Your systems. As James Clear says, "You do not rise to the level of your goals. You fall to the level of your systems" (2018, 27).

A system is an established procedure that outlines the actions needed to accomplish a task, and schools are full of them. We have systems for taking attendance, administering discipline, entering grades, contacting parents, fixing technology, and so much more. You may have complex systems, like the gauntlet of budget approval committees; niche systems, like the flowchart managing precise emergency communication procedures; and nebulous systems, like the mysterious black box into which suggestions for improvement seem to disappear.

Let me ask you this: How do new teachers in your district learn about your systems? Do you assume mentors cover these things? Do you figure department chairs probably find time to address them in a meeting at some point? Do you tell new teachers to ask a colleague to learn how to look up a phone number or provide sub plans or renew their teaching license? Maybe so. More than likely, that was how you learned the ropes during your first teaching job. You asked the person next door where to find resources, you stayed late teaching yourself how to use technology, and you did what everyone else seemed to be doing during parent conferences.

Look at things from a current new teacher's perspective, though. In an age when all information in the known world can be summoned in a millisecond using the phone in your pocket, it's ludicrous that anyone has to ask their neighbor how to post a sub plan—and even more ludicrous that we think the neighbor's time is well-spent teaching this menial task.

Look, too, at the sheer volume of chores teachers must perform compared to the scanty time we allot for task-oriented training. Teachers might spend 50 percent of their day attending to basic procedures, but leaders barely spend 5 percent of induction time teaching these duties. Let's face it: we make the first few years of teaching unnecessarily cumbersome by not having our systems in order. We squander new staff orientation time with philosophical lectures and leave the teaching of concrete tasks to tribal knowledge. As a result, teachers waste time scrambling to find information and teach themselves procedures that we should have laid out.

Consider the facts. Rarely do districts devote orientation time to showing teachers how to complete basic procedures, such as calling home, taking attendance, requesting supplies, or entering discipline. Even more rarely do they have a library of instructional videos on key technological platforms, such as the student information system or the learning management system, for teachers to access during those harrowing first weeks when everything is a crisis. Rarest of all are districts who commit serious time for new teachers to learn the curriculum; most simply tell teachers where to find it and ask their mentor if they have questions.

In a perversely common summary of her induction, one teacher points to the lack of practical instruction:

> It was weird. You really can't call what I experienced induction; it was more like a trial by fire. I came into the school all enthusiastic and ready to go, but within days it seemed I was left on my own. I didn't know what programs I was teaching, where I could get resources—it was really hard. I made it through those first few months by working ten to twelve hours a day. The other teachers said they would help but they had their own classes and looked just as busy as I was so I felt bad asking for help. I felt like a failure in those first few months. (Kearney 2016)

Imagine not knowing what programs you're supposed to teach or where you can find resources. Imagine, too, the very real possibility that "resources" are a figment of your imagination, that no materials have been curated for your learning. Compound all that with the implied assumption that tribal knowledge will save the day. This is what most teachers can expect from their orientation. Then, too, there is a disconnect between what leaders value and what teachers value. The most crucial issues to new hires are often things we deem unworthy of our attention, such as technological snafus or classroom setup.

When we ignore new teachers' hierarchy of needs, we set them up for failure. How is anyone supposed to focus on a motivational speech when he can't log into his computer? Who cares about an HR lecture when she hasn't been allowed to see her classroom? It's true that you, as a school leader, may not have the expertise to solve every problem yourself, but your onboarding system should have solutions to common problems available immediately—as in, right then and there, during orientation.

If you were the new teacher who couldn't log into his computer at orientation, for instance, you'd be furious if your principal responded with, "Ask your mentor to help you submit a tech support request." *On what device? You can't log in! Your mentor may not know to bring her computer!* When will you even meet this mentor, anyway? On the other hand, imagine hearing your principal say, "Our tech support team is here right now. I'll walk you over to their station so they can fix this." You'd be grateful that your leaders anticipated the issues that are the most important to you—like being able to use your most important work tool.

Planning induction without considering teachers' perspectives means we prioritize the wrong things. We drag recruits through compliance training to cover our you-know-whats. We give rambling, philosophical lectures in a misguided effort to establish high expectations. We conduct cringey icebreakers, thinking this is the way to build a warm culture.

Teachers hate this. Wouldn't you? And yet, we act like boring, irrelevant, feckless orientations are unavoidable, when actually, we have the power to make them engaging, personalized, and targeted to educators' immediate needs. Even better, we have the power to make that first year of teaching productive rather than torturous.

Teachers need a practical plan in order to excel during their first year, with a curated list of the basic tools and procedures their school uses. This would inspire them with more confidence than any motivational speech delivered by a well-meaning superintendent. It would allow them to spend their time focusing on instruction rather than on finding answers to simple questions, thus making them more effective and more satisfied.

And yet, very few districts have an on-demand library of fully articulated systems sitting on a website, ready for new employees to peruse as part of their induction process. To those outside education, the idea of a systems library feels like mere common sense. To administrators in the trenches, however, it feels like an absurd pipe dream. Here's why:

1. It takes serious time and energy to compile every system teachers need to master—not just to verbally recap them but to write, film, or illustrate them so they can be published and available on-demand.
2. Turnover is just as high among educational leaders as it is among teachers, meaning that few stick around long enough to see such a project all the way through. Additionally, incoming leaders may have positional authority to change existing systems, complicating the whole process.
3. Your school or district may not have consensus on what each system is in the first place, necessitating meetings, emails, and lengthy calibration discussions for which leaders don't always have time.
4. Streamlining and publishing systems never feels as important as large-scale innovation or drastic school improvement plans.

No wonder we don't have better induction. These are truly daunting obstacles to creating the sort of systems library we all want. This isn't a task for a spare afternoon, but rather, a multiyear project that will need continual maintenance. If you invest the time, however, you will see worthy dividends.

Your administrators, department chairs, mentors, and coaches will spend less time each year answering procedural questions and can focus instead on culture, instruction, and more. New teachers themselves will experience a smoother transition into your district, feeling less frustration and more confidence. Veteran teachers, who rightly complain about inconsistent answers from leadership, will appreciate the clarity and consistency of common systems. The benefit to your school, moreover, is obvious: well-maintained systems generate more faithful implementation, thus reducing the time leaders spend correcting erroneous behavior.

If that doesn't convince you to embark on this project, consider this: when asked why they leave a job or the profession, teachers cite many of the reasons we expect—compensation, social respect, and so on—but they also cite "lack of support" from districts, even those which feature professional learning communities (PLC) and mentoring programs (Economic Policy Institute 2019). The Learning Policy Institute reports that "the workplace condition most predictive of teacher turnover was a perceived lack of administrative support" (Carver-Thomas and Darling-Hammond 2017).

How can this be? We, as leaders, always *feel* eager to support new teachers, but realistically, is our money where our mouth is? Have we set up the concrete systems needed to support new teachers—the things they actually *want*? Clearly not, if teachers still feel unsupported.

Making our support visible, applicable, and omnipresent can bridge the gap between leaders' good intentions and teachers' actual needs. That bridge starts with a firm grasp of what constitutes a good system, at least as far as it applies to the teaching profession. This will help leaders tailor a systems library for new teachers. For our purposes, good systems are

- Practical: grounded in recurring, concrete, necessary tasks
  - Focusing on the practical acknowledges the sheer volume of tasks teachers do on a daily basis and sets them up for immediate material success. Moreover, starting your systems library with practical matters frees you and your team up to focus on culture and pedagogy later once you have the procedural nuts and bolts in place.
- Published: accessible on-demand
  - Putting your systems library on a website, for example, eliminates human error. A new teacher could ask five people the same question and receive five different answers. An on-demand system ensures consistency. It guarantees an immediate, correct answer.
- Promoted: advertised, utilized, and valued
  - Incorporating your systems library into induction is essential to its success. No one wants such an invaluable resource to collect digital dust in a corner of the district website. That's why every leader in the district must adopt the habit of talking about the systems library at every turn, especially when interacting with new teachers.

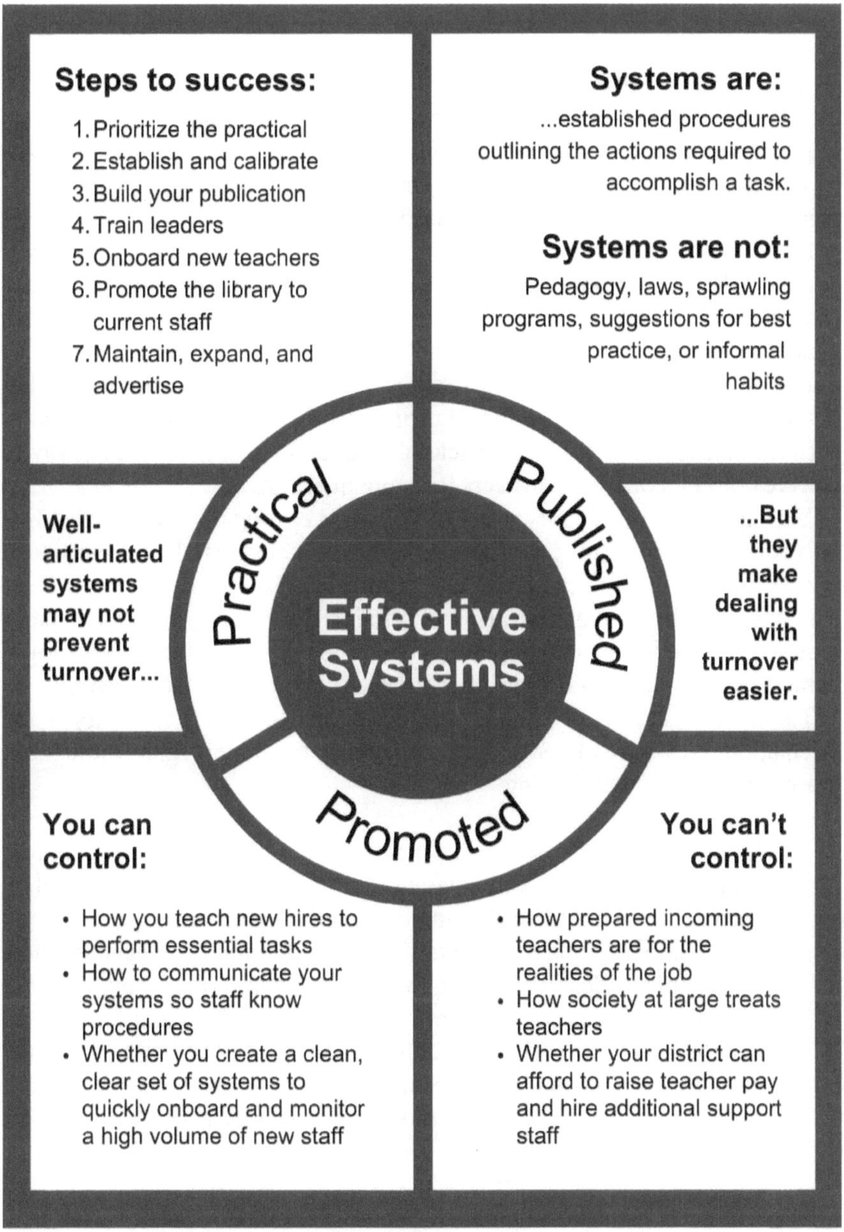

Steps to success:

1. Prioritize the practical
2. Establish and calibrate
3. Build your publication
4. Train leaders
5. Onboard new teachers
6. Promote the library to current staff
7. Maintain, expand, and advertise

Systems are:

...established procedures outlining the actions required to accomplish a task.

Systems are not:

Pedagogy, laws, sprawling programs, suggestions for best practice, or informal habits

Well-articulated systems may not prevent turnover...

Effective Systems

Practical • Published • Promoted

...But they make dealing with turnover easier.

You can control:

- How you teach new hires to perform essential tasks
- How to communicate your systems so staff know procedures
- Whether you create a clean, clear set of systems to quickly onboard and monitor a high volume of new staff

You can't control:

- How prepared incoming teachers are for the realities of the job
- How society at large treats teachers
- Whether your district can afford to raise teacher pay and hire additional support staff

Figure I.1. Overview of effective systems.

Figure I.1 illustrates how the three P's of good systems function in the large scheme of school turnover, and it lists the seven steps this book recommends to leaders who want to organize, calibrate, and communicate clean systems to increasing numbers of new staff.

Let's envision how this might look next August. You have a large cohort of incoming teachers—a mix of fresh-faced college grads and veterans transferring from other districts. These new hires get three orientation days, followed by two institute days with the staff at large, and immediately after that, a barrage of students flood the school halls. Time is precious.

If you give yourself permission to abandon counterproductive practices, you cut a lot of fat from the usual orientation schedule: motivational speakers, compliance training, and icebreakers, for a start. (We'll talk about where to address necessary evils, such as compliance training, later on in the book.) Every second of your remaining time must build toward one goal: quickly build teachers' proficiency in the recurring, necessary tasks they will need to perform during the first month of school, and familiarize them with a way to receive correct, consistent answers to future questions.

You have a systems library ready; it's a robust catalog of resources that live on your district website. Clear categorial headers such as "Learn daily tech tasks," "Explore the curriculum," and "Connect with parents" tell new hires where to look for information, and each section has an easily navigable list of topics. Some topics include how-to videos, while others feature short, simply phrased written descriptions of procedures. It's focused on the *practical.*

The library isn't simply a tool used during orientation. The library *is* the orientation. New hires interact with the library again and again throughout those three days of onboarding:

- Not only do you show teachers where to find family contact information, you have them actually call a parent to introduce themselves. Now, they have practiced both the technological and the social skills.
- Not only do you explain where to find the curriculum, you have teachers grade sample student work using the district rubrics. Now, they know the standards they're teaching and also how to assess proficiency.
- Not only do you provide classroom setup time, but you also distribute checklists, guidelines, and training on physical setup via the library. Now, teachers can set up their rooms purposefully and efficiently. It's *published* so it can be used as a learning tool.

You can even gamify the process. Scavenger hunts or pop quizzes may challenge teachers to find answers to common questions using the systems library, and a badging program can award and incentivize the mastering of each system. Since you only have three days of orientation, you prioritize the systems teachers need to internalize to succeed during their first month in the classroom, but you make sure they know exactly how and where to find information needed later in the year. Remember, the goal is to build confidence, and a key part of that is helping teachers help themselves.

All district mentors and administrators are fluent in the systems library, and when new teachers ask for help with basic tasks, they provide this help using library resources. It's *promoted* by all internal leaders.

By following the three P's of good systems, school and district leaders can maintain stability throughout otherwise turbulent times. This method anticipates and prepares for turnover in a direct, transparent way, and it puts you, the educational leader, in charge. Imagine a future where turnover doesn't bother you because you know you have an excellent onboarding program, one that makes teachers' first year less harrowing.

In that future, you'd have a different attitude toward staffing altogether. You wouldn't feel desperate and fearful each spring, dreading the flood of resignations; rather, you'd feel eager to make sure every employee was truly a good fit, truly reaching his or her potential, and if not, you could be confident in your ability to set the next person up for success in a smoothly operating ecosystem.

If you feel like you're up against the ropes, trying to thrive despite never-ending staff changes, this book is for you. If you want advice on how to get a grip on things you definitely can control, as opposed to the myriad things you can't, this book is for you. By all means, read the literature on staff culture—a significant predictor of team success—and on multiplying the capacity of your team even with limited human capital. Those are excellent resources, and they can round out your understanding of the issue of teacher retention.

This book, however, assumes that turnover *will* happen, at least for the foreseeable future, and it focuses on how to keep your school functioning despite this harsh reality. The benefit to leaders, moreover, is obvious: well-maintained systems generate more faithful implementation, thus reducing the time leaders spend correcting erroneous behavior. Each chapter will provide planning templates, which you can replicate for your own work, as well as guiding questions to help you start the dialogue with your colleagues.

Step 1

Prioritize the Practical

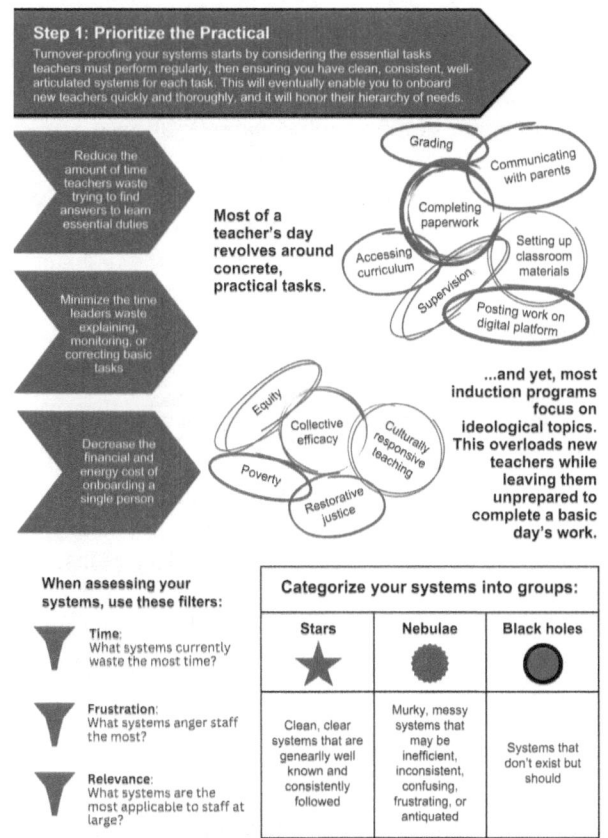

Figure 1.1. Prioritize the practical.

WHERE TO START AND WHY

With so many factors to consider, from equity to safety to learning loss, why should you prioritize the establishment of practical systems, especially as a response to turnover? It's actually very simple: to save time.

Time is our most valuable resource. It is, as Benjamin Franklin said, "the stuff life is made of," and the majority of a teacher's time is spent completing concrete tasks: handling materials, managing classes, and communicating information. Despite this, schools exert astonishingly little energy maintaining systems for these tasks, focusing instead on philosophical aims. This is a source of consternation, particularly among new teachers—after all, it's hard to think about ideology if you can't connect to a printer.

Wasted time should anger leaders. You want your teachers to spend their prep periods planning targeted instruction or providing constructive feedback to students, not hunting down the answer to a policy question. You, yourself, want to spend your days improving instruction and supporting students, not reteaching every new hire how to contact parents, and yet you can't ignore these fundamental tasks.

Therefore, you must create a way for staff to instantly access accurate information without relying on the dubious institution of tribal knowledge. If the goal is to free up time for more important things, the first step is to reduce the amount of time spent searching for and learning concrete tasks. That's why you must prioritize the practical.

GET OUT OF THE TOWER AND INTO THE TRENCHES

Wasted time is never just about time. It's about the pride a district takes in operating smoothly and the attention school leaders pay to supporting teachers. It's about the education students receive from effective instructors, whose time is respected and whose success is enhanced.

Consider the seemingly simple issue of leaving lesson plans for a substitute teacher. Your school might require lessons to be posted on a learning management system (LMS), submitted to the school secretary, or simply left on the teacher's desk. What could possibly go wrong?

Just for a start:

- The sub may not know how to use the learning management system
- Students may not be able to access the LMS due to uncharged devices
- The copier may be too swamped with teachers for the secretary to copy materials in the morning

- Students or staff may have unknowingly moved the plans from the teacher's desk
- Students may treat the lesson as a "free day" in the teacher's absence, feigning ignorance when the substitute teacher explains the lesson
- The lesson itself may be poor, involving mere busywork

This everyday issue isn't just about time. It's also about lost education for students, low morale for substitutes, and probably behavior referrals for administration. Consider, too, the teacher's frustration upon returning to learn that a class did nothing because of some preventable mishap.

Shoddy, unclear systems suggest that school leadership can't be bothered with the day-to-day realities of education—and all too often, they can't. The dirty, if open, secret is that districts usually end up with messy systems as a result of revolving-door administration. Every incoming leader has the potential to upend existing systems, changing the rules at a moment's notice, and erasing everyone's past efforts.

Then, too, school and district leaders often expend all their energy on new initiatives, rather than keeping the nuts and bolts into place. This is, after all, what leaders study in graduate school: change theory, organizational development, and so on. It's also how administrators are evaluated: how well they generated improvements and transformed culture. Focusing on grand innovations, while important, can shift leaders' attention away from the things that consume staff time and energy.

If leaders live in an ivory tower, oblivious to the realities of teaching, the problem isn't just about the time, it's about the chasm between administrators and teachers and the perceived lack of consideration for the tasks that make schooling happen. Teachers are right to lament their mounting pile of tasks. They're also right to feel insulted by unclear, wasteful, or ineffective systems upheld by apathetic leaders.

It's all very well to apply lofty leadership theory to your work but not at the expense of your team's basic functionality. How can teachers take your grand philosophizing about pedagogy, culture, and equity seriously if you don't care enough to make the nuts and bolts fall into place?

ASSESS THE WASTE

Ultimately, turnover hurts because it involves so much waste: wasted time, wasted money, wasted energy. It's "waste," not "investment" because, bluntly put, the new hire may quit within the first five years, as 44 percent do (University of Pennsylvania 2018). This makes the $20,000 average sticker price of recruiting and onboarding a new employee all the more appalling

(Learning Policy Institute 2017). That's why any effort to confront turnover head on should focus primarily on reducing waste. You're trying to build an onboarding structure that does the following:

- Reduces the time teachers waste trying to find answers or learn essential duties
- Minimizes the time leaders waste explaining, monitoring, or correcting basic tasks
- Decreases the financial and energy cost of onboarding a single person

A structure that achieves these aims *will* require an investment, but you will be investing in yourself and your organization, not in any individual employee. You'll spend considerable time upfront assembling your systems library, and you will reap the benefits throughout the year—even years—when you have more time to focus on developing culture, supporting instruction, and building relationships.

To start the process, you need to assess where time, energy, and money are spinning down the drain. The best information will come from your staff—specifically from new teachers, mentors, and administrators. The first people to involve are your recent hires. Survey teachers in their first, second, or third year in the district as to what ate up their excess time when they first started.

The key here is to focus their answers on practical systems, not personal anxieties. New teachers naturally overthink their decisions and stress about minor problems, and no elegant systems library can provide a guaranteed remedy to that. However, new teachers can tell you where their biggest frustration points were: information they wish had been readily available, questions to which they received several different answers, and procedures they had to beg their neighbors to teach them.

If you are in the earliest phases of refining new teacher induction, or if you simply need a general idea of how teachers perceive your onboarding program, an open-ended survey would be most useful. Consider table 1.1, which invites new staff to provide insight and suggestions.

If, on the other hand, you have a solid set of skills you seek to build in new teachers and merely want a sense of how effectively you build them, consider

Table 1.1.

Question	Answer
How useful was the information provided during new staff induction?	
What should we have spent more time on?	
What should we have spent less time on?	
Did you feel prepared for the first week of school? What helped?	

table 1.2, which is a Likert scale asking teachers to self-assess. This tool provides information on teachers' confidence and competence, and it helps you gauge which practical skills to teach more explicitly. This table includes example skills for illustrative purposes:

Mentors are also a potent source of information. Simply learning what tasks each mentor taught his mentee will provide insight. You might reveal inconsistencies between mentors, with some covering more tasks than others, or you may discover that mentors are not covering everything you thought they would, leaving gaps in your overall induction. Alternatively, you may discover that mentors spend an unreasonable amount of time picking up the slack from a haphazard new staff orientation; if, for example, mentors barely have time to focus on instruction due to the need to teach procedures, you know there's an imbalance.

You want to get an accurate picture without making mentors feel tripped up. Frame whatever questions, surveys, or interviews you posit as a simple needs assessment, a way to ascertain what topics are covered and where the school can be more proactive.

Building-level administrators also have a front row seat to inefficiency and waste, although they may feel uncomfortable discussing it at first. Acknowledging gaps in school and district systems triggers guilt, defensiveness, or irritation from an already-overworked principal, who wonders if he or she missed an email or slouched on a task. Still, though, administrators

Table 1.2.

Please rate your proficiency with each system			
	I cannot do this at all	I might be able to do this, but I'm not sure	I can definitely do this
Find and follow the curriculum for all my subjects or classes			
Navigate the student information system for daily tasks, including taking attendance and finding parent contact information			
Set up lessons on our digital learning management system and teach students how to use it			

can track and report things like the number of questions they receive around a common topic, the time they spend helping teachers learn basic systems, and staff adherence to required procedures.

The adherence issue can be the most revealing, and also the best way to get a reticent principal to open up. Asking, "What do you wish more staff did correctly?" can open the floodgates, and you may receive an earful of information about teachers miscalculating grades, botching the reimbursement request process, or coding discipline referrals inaccurately.

Table 1.3 is a simple tally sheet—nothing so onerous that a principal couldn't hang it next to his or her desk. It asks nothing more than a tally when systemic confusion requires a principal's attention. If principals used this for even the first week of school, the results could be invaluable. Again, examples are provided for illustrative purposes but could easily be substituted.

PRIORITIZE, PRACTICALLY

Now that you have ample data on how teachers, mentors, and administrators perceive your systems, your next step is to prioritize. Chances are, you've received an overwhelming amount of information and feedback, and applying some different filters to your findings will help you to parcel it into manageable chunks and help you to make a plan.

The first filter is *time*: What systems currently waste the most time? Why do they waste time? Maybe they are unclear or inefficient. Maybe they are inconsistently explained by leadership, leading to confusion. Maybe they rely on verbal explanations or tribal knowledge when a simple video tutorial would clarify. To apply the time filter to a system, ask these questions:

- Where is the wasted time coming from?
- Whose time is wasted?

Table 1.3.

System	Emails	Personal questions or conversations	Staff mistakes
Calculating and entering grades			
Setting up classrooms in accordance with school guidelines			
Establishing online content via the learning management system			

- What is the consequence of the wasted time?
- What would an improved model look like?
- Who needs to be involved in order to make the improvement?

The next filter is *frustration*: what systems anger staff the most? Why do they incite anger? Perhaps they are unnecessarily litigious or full of bureaucratic red tape. Perhaps they are inconsistently enforced by leadership, making them appear silly. They might be futile, requiring staff to complete tasks for no real purpose and with no actual result, or maybe the frustration comes from the very fact that these systems waste teachers' and leaders' precious time.

Consider, too, what the frustrated people are doing as a result of their anger. If they're complaining bitterly, cutting corners, or starting to flout the rules altogether, you have additional issues to untangle. To apply the frustration filter to a system, ask these questions:

- Where is the frustration coming from?
- Which groups are the most frustrated?
- What is the consequence of the frustration?
- What would an improved model look like?
- Who needs to be involved in order to make the improvement?

The third filter is *relevance*: what systems are the most applicable to staff at large? What will, if properly published and promoted, improve most people's experience at work? Maybe your improvements can simultaneously help teachers and administrators, and ideally, this work will have an impact on students. To apply the relevance filter to a system, ask these questions:

- Which groups of staff does this system impact?
- Does this have a ripple effect on students or families?
- How frequently is the system used throughout the year?
- What would an improved model look like?
- Who needs to be involved in order to make the improvement?

Your final step is to make a plan for the start of next school year. Using the August arrival of new staff as the annual deadline for updating your systems library helps you to pace yourself realistically. You won't be able to make a fully complete library by this August, no matter how motivated you are, so you need to categorize and prioritize.

The goal of categorizing is to determine the status of a system; in other words, how much work needs to be done before a given system can be confidently published. If your district is like most, you probably have a mix of clear and unclear, formal and informal, printed and assumed, enforced and unenforced systems, and creating a vivid picture of the status of each system will help you select a reasonable workload for fall. Below is one method you can use to categorize your current systems:

- Star systems are generally well known and consistently followed. They're clean and clear. They do not waste time or cause frustration, but they may be widely relevant. You may or may not have these in writing, but if you don't, it's easily remedied. Star systems are ready to be added to your library.
- Nebulae are systems that are murky or messy. They may be inefficient, inconsistent, confusing, frustrating, or antiquated. Whether or not you have these written out doesn't necessarily matter, because they have issues. A nebulous system requires some revision before you can publish it into a library.
- Black holes are systems that don't exist but should. They're the bane of a leader's existence, the project no one wants to touch. Maybe these systems existed in the past, but they were ineffective or poorly maintained, and they are now swirling in the vortex, fomenting confusion among staff who simply need to accomplish something.

Stars ★	Nebulae	Black holes
Systems that are generally well known and consistently followed	Systems that are inefficient, inconsistent, confusing, frustrating, or antiquated	Systems that should exist, but don't; the project no one wants to touch
"Our attendance, tardiness, and truancy system is very clean. All teachers know how to take attendance and do so, accurately and on time, and the system picks up multiple tardies and flags truants."	"Ok, if you want to apply for a leave of absence, it's about 45 steps... first, you have to find the paper form from the 80's, then you have to walk it over to HR in person, then they'll call your doctor, your lawyer, and your next of kin. It should take about a month."	"I'm honestly not sure what social media rules we even have... I think the last superintendent made some, but I don't know if they're still a thing. Maybe one of the principals would know?"

Figure 1.2. Status of systems.

If you are just starting to build a systems library, or if you are short on time and human capital, you may want to include plenty of star systems in order to build up steam and sell the value of the project to your colleagues. Showing other leaders a small but clean library of well-articulated systems will make the task seem manageable and attractive, whereas describing a hypothetical collection will make it seem like an unwieldy fantasy.

Prioritizing is the second part of your planning, and this allows you to determine which nebulae and black holes to tackle. You'll want to tackle at least one of these every year . . . otherwise what's the point? This is where Table 1.4 will come into play; if a nebulous system or a black hole checks all three boxes—it wastes time, causes frustration, and is widely relevant—it should be higher on your priority list.

As you prioritize, consider the feasibility of clarifying, revising, or inventing each system. In your current role, you may or may not have unilateral authority to fix everything needing attention. This doesn't mean you can't do anything, but it does mean you may have to enlist the help of those who do. For example, if you are a principal and want to help teachers understand the district business office's nebulous expense reimbursement system, prepare to be assertive. You'll have to set up meetings, suggest improvements to people who don't want to hear them, and take on the tedious work of pushing a committee toward consensus.

Another aspect of feasibility is time: realistically, how long will it take to make the needed changes? For every person involved and every layer of review, lengthen your time frame. Remember your goal of showcasing a systems library to new and veteran staff this fall, and select projects that can be achieved by August.

PUT IT ALL TOGETHER

This is your action plan: the guiding document to determine which systems you will clarify, revise, or invent for next year. These systems will be the first additions in your library. Publishing and promoting them will help your onboarding of new staff, but veterans, too, will appreciate their clarity and

Table 1.4.

System	Wastes time	Causes frustration	Widely relevant

Table 1.5.

System	Category Star, nebula, or black hole?	Priority How many boxes does this check?	Feasibility Do I have power and time to streamline?	Involved parties Who will make decisions, who will review?	Will I tackle this for next fall?

the convenience of accessing them. Table 1.5 will help you synthesize your assessment information, and you can use it as your springboard into Step 2.

SUMMARY

- Time is our most valuable resource, and squandering it angers people.
- Wasted time isn't just about time. It's about morale, perception, and lost opportunity.
- New teachers, mentors, and administrators can tell you where they're wasting the most time.
- Their insight will help you make a starting list of systems for your library.
- Apply filters of time, frustration, and relevance to determine what systems should take priority.
- Categorize your systems into stars, nebulae, and black holes to predict how much attention they require before they can be included in the library.

Start the Dialogue

Questions to Start the Work with Your Colleagues

1. What are the tasks teachers must be able to perform correctly within their first month on the job?
2. What do we currently do to make sure they can perform these tasks? What checks for understanding do we implement?
3. In what ways do we leave teacher learning to chance? For instance, are there tasks we *assume* they learn from their mentors or gather via tribal knowledge?
4. What data would help us better understand how effectively we prepare teachers for the tasks they must perform during their first month?

Step 2

Establish and Calibrate

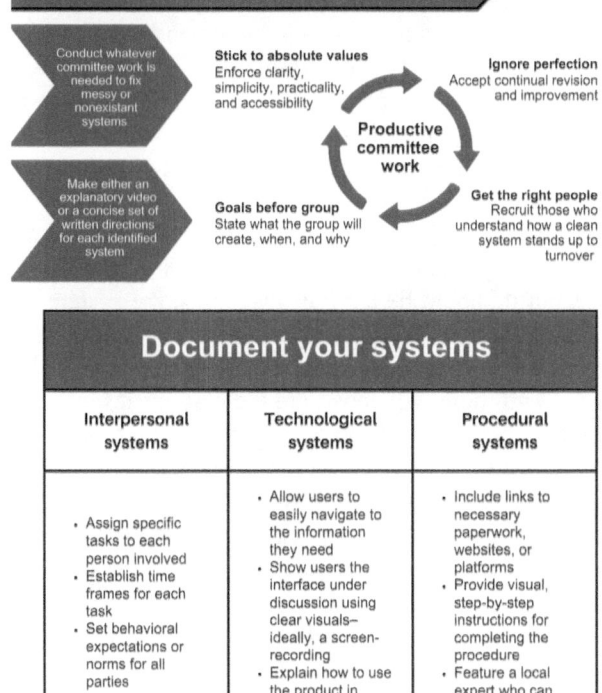

Figure 2.1. Establish and calibrate.

CLARIFY, REVISE, OR INVENT THE RIGHT SYSTEMS TO WITHSTAND TURNOVER

In the last chapter, you established a list of systems to include in your library. Next, you'll create a very specific product: for each system on your action plan, you will make either a clear, concise set of written directions or a short explanatory video.

The goal of these written or recorded directions is to teach a newcomer how to follow the system. Some will be simple and task oriented; for instance, a one-minute video demonstrating how to enter grades. Others will be complex and multilayer; for instance, a handbook explaining the student discipline system.

Here's the rub: it's not always as easy as extracting the knowledge from your head. As we established in chapter 1, your district probably has a mix of solid and shaky systems, so you'll have to clarify, revise, or outright invent some systems before you can put them in writing. This chapter will provide a framework for the clarification, revision, and invention of systems.

Your labeling of systems will determine your first step. Remember, the labels indicate the status of each system—in short, how fully formed, well known, and faithfully observed it is.

Star systems, which are well known and consistently followed, probably just need minor clarification or better publishing. If a clear set of written guidelines or video directions does not exist for these systems, invest the small amount of time to make one. You can do this yourself or delegate to a team member, but it should be a minor task since the system itself is fairly solid. There's no need to construct an elaborate committee to reinvent the wheel; a few dedicated people can crank out written or recorded explanations for star systems, and these will constitute the first entries into your library.

You might be wondering why a star system, which is well known and consistently followed, even needs to be published in the systems library. One reason is time: every published system saves time for your mentors, administrators, and new teachers, who can simply refer to a link on demand, rather than go through a verbal explanation during those chaotic first weeks of school.

Equally important, though, is resilience: just because a system is well known and followed *now* doesn't mean it will always be that way. If you've been in education long enough, you've witnessed seemingly solid practices fall apart the moment someone stops monitoring them, either due to leadership changes or to competing priorities.

Even if you, personally, intend to stay in your district for a while, it's in your best interest to protect the resilience of the system; think about how frustrating it would be to learn that a new principal in another building is giving different directions about procedures than you are, or how upset you would be to discover that staff had ceased to follow the rules which you had assumed were ingrained and subsequently stopped monitoring. Having a common library makes your systems resilient over time and less subject to personal interpretation.

Nebulous systems, which are murky or messy, require more finagling. Examining why the system is nebulous, and how it came to be so unclear, will help you determine how to proceed. Systems become nebulous when:

- They are so inefficient or frustrating that people *don't* follow them
- They are so confusing or poorly documented that people *can't* follow them
- They are inconsistently enforced by those in authority, making people doubt their importance
- They have changed over time without proper communication

To fix a nebulous system, you need to root out the source of the mess. You probably have a hunch, but make sure to cross-reference this with your interviews, surveys, and data from chapter 1, and to ask for more information if needed. You're trying to make a one-sentence goal, such as, "We will eliminate unnecessary paperwork from our tech support system" or "We will ensure that all principals enforce the materials checkout process consistently."

Depending on your position, you may or may not have the authority to single-handedly create a clean system from a nebula and enforce it as law. Chances are, though, you'll need to enlist the participation of at least a few other people in order to revise a confusing system.

Say, for example, that your district's teacher evaluation system is clear on the basics—who fills out what form and when—but hazy on answers to common questions. What rating triggers an improvement plan? What should a teacher do if he disagrees with the rating? What if there is no evidence to support any rating at all?

Evaluators run into these questions frequently, so districts would be wise to publish clear answers in a common location for everyone's benefit. Fixing this nebulous system, however, requires collaboration from HR, administration, and teacher representatives. Your job is to be the facilitator; you're gathering the right people into a room to revise the system, so that you can confidently publish and promote it.

Then there are black holes—the systems that should exist but don't. Black holes develop when the following happens:

- A program, problem, or system is not the responsibility of any one person and falls into disuse

- An issue is ignored indefinitely because fixing it will be tedious and complicated
- Incoming leaders dismantle old systems without implementing clear replacements

Addressing a black hole is a challenge, no doubt about it. What's worse, though? Sitting through some exasperating meetings or shrugging your shoulders while staff stew in frustration? As with nebulae, black holes require analysis of the root cause of the problem, and you may receive wildly different accounts from teachers, secretaries, administrators, and central office.

For example, perhaps your district's social media practices are a black hole. Teachers and principals set up accounts for their classes and buildings with—apparently—no common guidelines. There are no published rules that anyone is aware of, and each building seems to have different de facto practices, with secretaries taking the lead in some schools, principals in others. When you ask central office administrators about this, you learn that guidelines were created under the last superintendent, but no one is sure if they still apply. There isn't a communications director, so it's not the job of any specific person to wrangle this issue under control.

You can see, however, that a lack of social media guidelines is a recipe for disaster, so you decide to do something about it. This is a tricker project than simply tidying up an existing system; in this case, you'll have to create something from nothing. Since social media is no one's sole responsibility—least of all yours—you'll need to enlist help from a variety of district representatives and get the blessing of someone in a position of high authority.

Black holes, like nebulae, necessitate committee work, which can be a blessing or a curse. On one hand, you need different perspectives represented when making revisions or new creations. On the other, they can be tense, tedious, or futile. That's why you can employ a few simple techniques to ensure a productive group effort.

AVOID DEATH BY COMMITTEE

Yes, you need representatives from key stakeholder groups, but you also want to make decisions in time for them to matter. Undoubtedly, you've suffered the agonizingly slow progress of a dysfunctional committee that over-complicated a simple project, resulting in a feckless, unremarkable product. If you don't want to spend a year analyzing every word choice and considering every obtuse hypothetical, take these preemptive steps:

- *Put the goals before the group.* Before you assemble your team, state this in writing:
  - Exactly what the group will create
  - The hard deadline for creation
  - Why the task must be accomplished by the deadline
  - Example: "This committee will create written guidelines for student discipline. It will outline the behavior management techniques teachers should use in class, as well as the conditions under which they should send students out of the classroom. It will also explain our school's categorization of student misbehavior and the consequences for each category. These written guidelines will be complete by August 1, so that they can be explained to new staff."

Put these written goals in front of every prospective group member *before* enlisting them. Anyone who agrees to participate on the committee agrees to uphold the goals. This may seem counterintuitive, given the amount of leadership theory devoted to building consensus and team spirit, but remember, this is a task-based group. It's not your school /improvement team, your climate and culture crew, or the parent-teacher organization. You're here to make a single, practical product, not to overhaul every aspect of teaching and learning. You can save hours of needless debate with a few clearly stated goals.

- *Stick to absolute values.* Write, state, and hold the committee accountable to these values:
  - Clarity: we will phrase this system in straightforward language
  - Simplicity: we will include only necessary steps, rules, or information
  - Practicality: we will consider how this system functions when applied in real life
  - Accessibility: we will make this system readily available to groups who need it

In practice, this means coming back to these values at the start of every meeting and referencing them throughout the process. If committee members begin to derail or overcomplicate the process, it's your job to remind them of the values of clarity, simplicity, practicality, and accessibility. You will become ever more skilled at finding ways to keep the work focused. You can suggest keeping a running list of hypotheticals to consider, knots to untangle, or questions to answer. You can put team members in charge of enacting their own suggestions, rather than adding to your own task list. You can use the values to ever-so-politely decline unhelpful ideas. Combined with your stated goals, the values can help create a usable system where none exists.

- *Get the right people.* The right people:
  - Understand how practical, published, promoted systems contribute to the district's functioning
  - Care about new teachers' successful onboarding experience
  - Can embrace your values despite the potentially complicated nature of creating a system

Ideally, you will gather a group large enough to represent the various roles impacted by your system. For instance, if you were creating a system for student discipline, you might involve a dean, a principal, a teacher, a counselor, and a parent. You want the committee to be small enough to create the system efficiently but large enough to incorporate all relevant perspectives. You also want to build a group with excellent social capital, which Michael Fullan and Joanne Quinn define as "the quality and quantity of interactions and relationships within the group," and to which they credit a group's "commitment to work together for a common purpose" (2016, 54).

- *Do not let perfect be the enemy of good.* Consistently remind the team of these things:
  - This is the first draft. You are creating something from nothing.
  - The system will have some room for improvement no matter how long you take to create it.
  - The system can—and should—be updated every year based on feedback from users.

This may be the hardest part. The conscientious, success-oriented people you've assembled will naturally want to create the best product possible, but too many committees stymie their own progress by obsessing over every minute detail until they lose sight of the overall goal.

Don't let this happen. With your committee, establish a way for end users to provide feedback on the system once it's operational, and agree to update the system annually based on feedback. This agreement allows you to see the system as "Plan A," and it helps you to resolve debates more quickly. Trying to decide between two ideas? Try one for next year and see how it goes. Worried about how staff will receive a new policy? Set up a digital suggestion box where they can offer ideas. Viewing the system as an ongoing practice, rather than an untouchable artifact, will keep the team on track.

Get a timeline in order from the first meeting and make visual trackers to indicate your progress. For example, you might employ a master checklist and cross off tasks the committee has already achieved. This could be created

Effective Committee Work

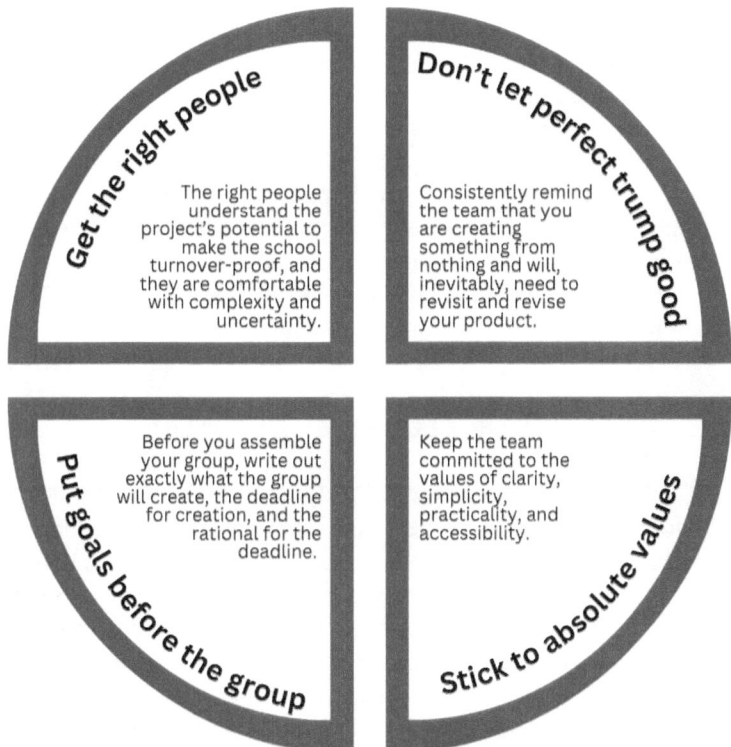

Figure 2.2. Effective committee work.

by the committee itself at the onset of the project, or it could be something you share with potential members as you enlist them, just like the goals.

Finally, it's your responsibility, as the facilitator, to keep the work focused by redirecting unproductive discussion. This could be everything from off-task chatter to proverbial wrenches thrown into the machine by ornery committee members. When someone tries to turn the discussion to an unlikely hypothetical, or to add an obsessive amount of unnecessary detail, or to undermine the overall project, redirect it. Come back to the goals, the timeline, or the refrain that this is a first draft. Talk to the committee member in private, if need be.

Running a committee doesn't have to be exasperating, but given that it will at least be time consuming, limit how many nebulae and black holes you take on each year. For the first iteration of the library, be realistic about how many systems you will be able to revise or invent, and lean on your committee members to help you achieve the work.

Table 2.1 demonstrates an agenda you could use for the first meeting dedicated to clarifying, revising, or inventing a system. It features an example system for illustrative purposes.

Table 2.2 is a simpler discussion template to use when evaluating the status of any system, whether interpersonal, technological, or procedural. You can use this in conjunction with the example committee meeting agenda (2A), or independently. The purpose of this template is to establish what is *known* about a system, including both what works and what doesn't, and to establish what is *assumed* about a system—that is, the things leaders *suppose probably happen* but can't prove. Having this discussion helps clarify how thoroughly a system is followed and how well it is monitored.

WRITE OR RECORD THE SYSTEMS

The end goal of these discussions is, firstly, to establish your systems, and secondly, to document them. A mere backroom handshake in which a committee reaches consensus is not enough. An actual product documenting the newly clarified, revised, or invented system is essential for transferring theory to practice, and these products will form the content of the systems collection—in other words, they will become the volumes in the library.

Because of the complexity of systems, there is no one documentation format that will apply to everything, from "How to write an IEP" to "How to enter grades." To make your finished product useful and cogent, consider what type of system you're working with. Most educational systems are either interpersonal, technological, or procedural. This section will outline how to document each type of system thoroughly.

Interpersonal systems regulate the way people interact when meeting for a defined purpose. Teacher evaluation is an example of an interpersonal system. The interactions between teacher and evaluator are regulated by a set of rules: the rating metrics, the requirements for evidence, the duration of the observation, and often the exact questions asked during evaluative meetings are all set in place before the evaluation process even starts.

Districts have scores of other interpersonal systems; staff discipline, remediation programs, and school improvement planning are likely to be fairly concrete already, given how litigious they can be. Others, such as mentoring, coaching, co-teaching, and onboarding, are often hazier.

It's essential to publish and promote interpersonal systems to ensure consistency. Consider mentoring. New teachers should not be subject to a "mentor lottery," in which the experience varies wildly from person to person, one

Table 2.1.

Committee goal: This committee will create written guidelines for social media use—specifically, rules for any staff member posting to social media on behalf of district or school accounts. These rules will identify who may post to district/school accounts and define appropriate content. The committee will also ensure our compliance with state and federal laws regarding the posting of images of minors, and it will establish any necessary consent forms for parents. These written guidelines will be complete by April 1, so that parent notification and consent may be obtained before student registration begins.

Committee values:
- Clarity: we will phrase social media guidelines in straightforward language
- Simplicity: we will include only necessary steps, rules, or information
- Practicality: we will consider how social media guidelines impact administrators, teachers, and students
- Accessibility: we will make this system readily available to groups who need it, and we will vet it with appropriate stakeholders, including our board of education and our union

Initial meeting agenda:
- Describe current reality: what do we know about social media practices in the district?
- How many district-affiliated social media accounts do we have, and is there a registration system or master list for these?
- Who has access to district accounts?
- Do we have any rules regarding what content is acceptable to post?
- Do we have branding guidelines, and if so, are they consistently followed?
- Do users know about state and federal laws regarding posting names or images of minors?
- Describe ideal reality: what do we want social media practices to look like?
- Are we comfortable with our current management process for district-affiliated social media accounts?
- Are we satisfied with those who have access to our accounts?
- Can our rules regarding acceptable content be improved?
- Can our branding guidelines or our monitoring of their use be improved?
- How can we better understand, communicate, and adhere to state and federal laws regarding posting names or images of minors?
- Identify gaps: based on our discussion, what are the top priorities for this committee to address?
- What registration or management systems do we need to establish?
- What branding or acceptable content guidelines do we need to make?
- What laws do we need to research and communicate?

Action steps:
- Determine who will take what step to address each gap between our current and desired reality.
- Who will make rough drafts of rules or guidelines?
- Who will research laws?
- Who will talk to principals, coaches, and others who run district-affiliated social media?
- Determine a time frame for each step.

Next meeting:
- Each committee member will report on his or her action steps.
- The committee will discuss problem areas, dependencies, and any need for additional information.
- The committee will discuss how and when improved social media guidelines may be communicated with staff at large.

Table 2.2.

What we know		
What parts of this system are solidly functional? How do we know?	What parts of this system are dysfunctional? How do we know?	What can we do to keep the information coming in reliably?

What we assume		
Where are the unknowns with this system? What happens in the dark, without accountability or monitoring?	What are the risks associated with the unknowns? In other words, what could go wrong due to unclear procedures or lack of monitoring?	What do we need to establish in order to eliminate the "black box" of assumptions?

mentor observing and coaching his protege every week, the next barely finding time for a handshake. Mentors should follow published rules outlining frequency of meetings, monthly focus areas, tools for providing observational feedback, and so much more. Moreover, program leaders should have a plan for monitoring the system.

If this seems like micromanaging, consider the frustration teachers feel when they realize they have different experiences from mentor to mentor, from evaluator to evaluator, from co-teacher to co-teacher.

Good interpersonal systems do the following:

- Assign specific tasks to each person involved
- Establish time frames for each task
- Set behavioral expectations or norms for all parties

Table 2.3 provides a sample template you can use for documenting interpersonal systems. Examples are included for illustrative purposes. This template would be useful either as a written document or else as a planner for an informational video. The goal is to specify *who* does *what* and *when*, and to supplement this with additional resources. It's also a way to establish behavioral norms to which you can hold people accountable throughout the year.

Technological systems regulate how to use a particular device, platform, or piece of technology. In most districts, the student information system is the prime example. Student grades, attendance, and family contact information live on a digital platform in which all staff must be fluent. Other examples often include emergency alert apps, learning management platforms, and employee payroll systems.

Table 2.3.

System: School Improvement Planning Process

Norms for all School Improvement Team members:
- Be solution oriented
- Respect diverse perspectives
- Present a united front

Task	Time frame	Task owner	Resources
Assemble School Improvement Team by posting online application and interviewing candidates	March	Building principal	Online application
Meeting 1: Analyze school's academic and behavioral data	April	Building administration and School Improvement Team	• Links to academic and behavioral data • Analysis questions
Meeting 2: Brainstorm potential ways to improve student learning or behavior	May	Building administration and School Improvement Team	• Links to relevant research • Brainstorming templates
Meeting 3: Establish school improvement plan for upcoming year	June	Building administration and School Improvement Team	School improvement plan template
Meeting 4: Conduct monthly meetings to analyze progress	Once per month throughout school year	Building administration and School Improvement Team	Data analysis form

So many tasks revolve around technology, and yet leaders rarely create direct instruction showing staff how to use key tech tools. Something more important always hogs the spotlight; it feels wasteful to show new hires how to use the gradebook when they haven't even met their mentor (plus, their mentor will definitely get around to showing them the gradebook, right?).

Then, too, a single administrator likely doesn't have the time and knowledge to create instructional material for all technological systems. Teachers, however, are expected to know a veritable truckload of tech—the student information system, the learning management system, the training registration system, the employee attendance system, the license renewal system, the emergency alert system, and countless more—and leaving the teaching of these systems to tribal knowledge seems downright reckless.

Good technological systems do this:

- Allow users to easily navigate to the specific information they need
- Show users the interface under discussion using clear visuals—ideally, a screen recording
- Explain how to use the product in plain, simple language

Table 2.4 is a sample template for documenting a technological system. Because technological systems are best conveyed via simple how-to videos, this is written as a script. The idea here is to describe a technological system in plain, direct language with no additional "fluff." Since teachers' time is precious, they will respond best to videos that take less than one minute to watch and that focus on exactly one task. A short, clear screen recording that answers a burning question will be more welcome than a lengthy film with Hollywood production value but minutes of unnecessary filler.

Procedural systems outline exact steps needed to accomplish a duty or chore. Expense reimbursement is an example of a procedural system. Athletic coaches or club sponsors typically file some sort of paperwork to be reimbursed for travel costs, and organized districts outline this procedure in a clear, accessible manner. Other procedural systems include entering semester grades, completing compliance training, reserving school space, registering for professional learning, or filing for parental leave.

Procedural systems can be the most infuriating to a new teacher because they *must* be done (think about it: you can't *not* enter grades or complete compliance training), but they are often the least maintained and published. Leaders understandably divert attention to big picture initiatives, assuming someone else will attend to nitty gritty operations. The trouble comes when there is no clear plan for having "someone else" train new teachers in

Table 2.4.

How to view a student profile on the student information system

"To view a student profile, first log into the student information system, then click 'My class' in the upper right-hand corner. If you have more than one class in the system, select the period or grade level you wish to view. Now, scroll down to the student's name and click it. This will bring up the student's profile. The top part of the profile shows you the student's ID number, parent contact information, and address. The middle area shows you his or her academic information, including schedule and current grades. On the bottom, you can find any essential health information, including allergies and daily medications."

procedures. This is where leaders are most likely to rely on tribal knowledge. After all, new teachers all seem to figure things out in the end.

Good procedural systems do the following:

- Include direct links to necessary paperwork, websites, or technological platforms
- Provide visual, step-by-step instructions for completing the procedure
- Feature a local expert who can answer additional questions

Table 2.5 provides a sample template for documenting procedural systems. Examples are included for illustrative purposes. Again, this template would be useful either as a written document or else as a planner for an informational video. The goal is to verbally and visually outline the steps a staff member must take in order to achieve a basic process.

As you create volumes for your library, remember this: don't let perfect be the enemy of good. Clear communication means more to teachers than glossy production value, so spend your time on the substance, not the dressing. Getting functional, accurate drafts of key systems together in time for your

Table 2.5.

How to file for expense reimbursement	
Step	Links, notes, and resources
Step 1: Download the expense reimbursement form from the staff management system	Direct link to the expense reimbursement form
Step 2: Fill out the expense reimbursement form	• Link to a sample completed form • Note: If you don't know the right account number, leave it blank
Step 3: Have your direct supervisor sign the form	• If you are a teacher, please have your principal sign the form • If you are an athletic coach, please have the athletic director sign the form
Step 4: Submit the form via email or interoffice mail to the business department	Click here to email businessdept@sampledistrict.edu
Step 5: Look for the expense to be reimbursed within two pay periods	• If you are enrolled in direct deposit, you will see the money in your account along with your normal paycheck • If you receive paper checks, you will be issued a separate check alongside your paycheck
Please contact Mrs. Smith in the business department (msmith@sampledistrict.edu) with questions.	

next new teacher induction will go a long way to inspiring confidence in the district, and it will save new and veteran teachers time and frustration as they navigate your district's policies and procedures.

SUMMARY

- Depending how developed they are, your systems may require anything from a mere written summary to a ground-up invention.
- If committee work is required to revise or invent a system, establish clear goals and timeframes before enlisting solutions-oriented people.
- Document systems as you establish them, either in writing or via simple instructional videos.
- Focus on simplicity and clarity, not production value.

Start the Dialogue

Questions to Start the Work with Your Colleagues

1. What are our "star" systems—those which are easiest to document right now? What would be the best format for communicating these to new teachers?
2. Looking at our nebulous systems, what does each system need in order to become clearer and cleaner? Which one would benefit new teachers the most if we could clarify or revise it?
3. Do we have bandwidth to tackle a black hole for next school year? If so, which one?
4. What stakeholders need to be part of our discussions as we seek to fix nebulae and black holes?

Step 3

Build Your Publication

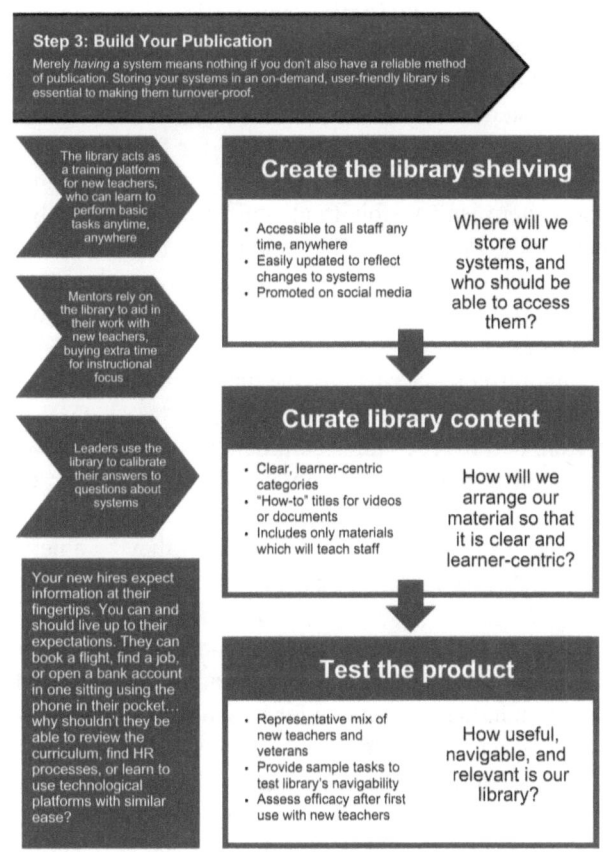

Figure 3.1. Build your publication.

HOW TO PUBLISH YOUR SYSTEMS ON THE ASSUMPTION THAT TURNOVER WILL HAPPEN

In the last chapter, you designed systems to withstand turnover. You constructed "volumes" for your library by clarifying, revising, or creating clean systems and writing or recording them in user-friendly language. Now, you will stock up your library shelves, organizing your work into a published product for staff.

This may be an essential step in the process, but it's the most easily overlooked. Many districts stop at simply *having* systems. They figure a committee convened and established something. Surely staff will follow along.

But how are staff supposed to learn the new system?

Are you sending an email? That's placing a lot of trust in people's speed reading and long-term retention. Are you assuming department chairs and building admin will relay the message? That's rolling the dice that the message will be consistent. Are you burying it in an HR file somewhere, just in case it's ever needed? That's setting people up for failure.

Having a system means nothing if you don't have a reliable method of publication. If the system isn't visible to all staff, they are unlikely to follow it. This can cause endless problems. The system may become meaningless, collecting dust on someone's hard drive. You may have given staff an ironclad excuse not to follow the system—after all, how are they supposed to follow rules that aren't posted anywhere?

Then, too, unpublished systems inflame the frustration felt by new teachers who want to learn the drill quickly but often have to ask a dozen colleagues the same question before receiving a confident answer. Your new hires expect information at their fingertips. You can and should live up to their expectations. They can book a flight, find a job, or open a bank account in one sitting using the phone in their pocket, so why shouldn't they be able to review the curriculum, find HR processes, or learn to use technological platforms with similar ease?

If you're trying to make your systems resilient to turnover, they must be published. This will allow you to use them as an onboarding tool, ensuring a smooth, hassle-free induction process for new hires. You need a publication.

A publication is a common location where all staff look for answers to systematic and procedural questions, a library that all staff can access—*and regularly do just that*. Imagine a digital place—a systems library—that is a household name in your district. It's organized into clear categories, so no one spends more than a few moments finding answers to questions or directions for systems.

For new teachers, the learning library is a vital onboarding tool, the thing that saves their mentors and them valuable time. For veteran teachers, it's a reassuring backbone of district procedures, the place to which they refer when unsure of how to complete specific tasks or address problems.

Every single employee of your district enters the learning library regularly; perhaps they are directed to read updated procedures at the start of each semester, or perhaps they use it to learn about new technology. If a teacher asks a colleague how to do something, the colleague makes sure his answer aligns with what's in the library. Why wouldn't he? All the right answers are outlined clearly in this one convenient location.

CREATE THE LIBRARY SHELVING

Your first—and most crucial—decision is where to locate your library. If you've been in education for decades, you may remember the days of the three-inch binder, complete with neatly labeled tabs. Every secretary's desk seemed to have one. Those were great resources for their time, but thank goodness, we no longer need to rely on paper copies of our systems!

Your library should be accessible to all staff at any time, day or night, from any location.

It should feature clear labels, so that staff can find what they need with minimal searching. It should be easily updated, so that midyear adjustments can be seamlessly reflected in the library. It should include *only* materials designed to teach systems. To be explicit, this is *not* the place to post every legalistic memorandum, disclaimer, contract, or set of terms and agreements. If it doesn't *teach people how to do something*, it doesn't belong in the library.

Here's why: you want the library to be so well-known and commonly used that the default response every staff member gives to procedural questions is this: "Have you checked the library?" It will never become such a thing if it is stuffed to the brim with extraneous documents that employees rarely need, forcing them to sift through useless clutter before finding what they want. Keep the legalistic codes of conduct, the memorandums of understanding, and the "CYA" documents in a separate location. The library is purely for teaching material. It should be clean, navigable, and useful.

By now, you're probably envisioning the library as a digital platform, which makes the most sense—this is the only way to meet the criteria of accessibility and easy updating. It could live on your district website, or else on whatever learning management system (LMS) you use for students' online learning.

Publishing your systems library on the district website has several advantages, most prominently, the website's ubiquity and accessibility. Chances are, staff already rely on the website for links to their email, employee portal, school calendars, tech support, and more—why not add the systems library to this existing hub? It makes access simple for staff by eliminating the need to add one more digital bookmark.

Alternatively, you might publish your systems library on your district's LMS, which has the benefit of teaching staff how to use the platform by turning them into learners. Teachers don't often have this experience, busy as they are setting up their digital classrooms. If they engage with the LMS-based library as a learner, they may gain insight into how the platform functions from a different perspective.

You might even consider relying on social media as a starting point or a supplement to your library; if you don't currently have the technological or human resources to post your systems on a website, you can post them on social media for now. Most social media platforms can support video and printed material, and they have the labeling and organizational capacity needed for a decent library.

Even if you do have a website-based library, social media can help to promote the product and enable real time discussion. Perhaps you create incentives for staff to follow your social media accounts, with giveaways and prizes posted only on these platforms. Perhaps you create on-the-fly answers to frequently asked questions, meaning that learners get immediate clarification.

One essential issue to consider when choosing where to publish your library is user access. To whom should your systems be viewable? Put another way, do you want the entire internet-connected world to be able to access your systems?

The answer might legitimately be *yes*. Maybe you want potential new hires to take one look at your website and be blown away by your seamless, thorough systems, which will make their induction smoother. The answer might just as legitimately be *no*. Maybe your systems include sensitive information or hard-won intellectual property that you simply do not wish to make available to one and all. In that case, consider requiring staff to log into a portal or intranet before they access that part of your website, or else, just use your LMS, which will inherently require a district account.

Table 3.1 provides a discussion guide that may help your team select a digital platform for your systems library.

CURATE CONTENT

Curation—the arrangement and labeling of content—will impact how users perceive your library, which will, in turn, impact how they use it. Remember,

Table 3.1.

What digital library platform best meets our needs?		
Question	Notes	Implications for library
What user groups *must* be able to access our library?		
Are we comfortable with nondistrict employees viewing some or all of our library?		
What is our district's current use of social media like? Would our staff view content posted or promoted through social media?		
What technological needs would we experience if we posted the library on our district website? Does our team have the capability to address these needs?		
What is current staff use of the LMS like? If we put the library on the LMS, will staff be more or less likely to engage with it than if we put the library on the website?		

this library should be clean, navigable, and useful. Every decision you make when organizing your content should contribute to this goal.

The first step is to decide on broad categories into which you can cluster your systems. The categories will be listed as headings on the main page of your library, allowing users to click through to the relevant content. As a leader, your mind may immediately jump to categories such as "HR," "Technology," and "Business," since these are the labels administrators use for district pillars. These are good starting points, but when you actually create your main page labels, you'll want to be more specific.

If your categories are too broad, you and other leaders will be tempted to add extraneous material that is not useful to staff. For example, if you have a "Technology" label, the Technology team may want to add everything from the acceptable use policy to the terms and conditions for every app used in the district, just for good measure. These documents do not belong in the library of systems, since they can compromise its cleanliness, navigability, and usefulness. The library is a teaching tool, not a repository of every dusty document administrators wish to purge from their files.

Your categories should be learner-centric, not district-centric. Learner-centric categories invite staff to an immersive, user-friendly learning experience, complete with content tailored to their exact needs. District-centric categories suggest that the administration has to cover its bases by posting legalistic disclaimers in a central location without actually caring about operations on the ground. Consider how the difference in phrasing may impact users:

Notice a pattern? Learner-centric categories

Table 3.2.

Learner-centric categories	District-centric categories
Learn to use district technology	District technology policies
Set your classroom up for success	Classroom setup expectations
Find answers from HR	Employee conduct and benefits
Get the most out of evaluations	Evaluation procedures

- Start with an imperative verb
- Have a positive connotation
- Imply active learning

When you phrase your categories in learner-centric language, your end product will come across as supportive, engaging, and relevant, and it will draw users in again and again.

Your next step is to set up your webpage, social media page, or LMS page to be visually appealing. This is where technology can really trounce the three-inch binder, as if you needed one more reason. An eye-catching main page simultaneously tells the user how to explore the library and entices him to do just that. It delivers on the promise of being clean, navigable, and useful.

If you don't have an extensive background in graphic design, don't worry. A few basic principles can make your library visually appealing:

- Keep it simple. Include only the most necessary information, and phrase it concisely. This applies to all areas of the library, but especially to the main page. Your main page probably needs a brief welcoming statement, a list of categories, and the email address of someone who can answer additional questions. That's it. It does not need elaborate philosophy, multipage flowcharts, or pictures scattered across every inch.
- Use district or school branding. Use the fonts, logos, and exact color codes for your district or school. This bestows an official atmosphere on the library, and it sends the message that the product is district-certified and reliable.
- Showcase the categories. Those learner-centric categories you just devised are the main navigational tool for users, so they should be front and center on your main page. Since each category will be hyperlinked to the content pertaining to it, you'll want to create a large, colorful button for each category—something that makes it prominent, appealing, and clear. Again, this is the most important part of your library, so nothing should be bigger, bolder, or more eye-catching than these categories. They are what draws users in.

How personally involved you are with the technological piece depends on your skill with web design, social media, or your district's LMS. You may need to enlist the help of your district's webmaster or communications team in order to physically create the actual page, but you should still go into that meeting with a design idea. Sketch your idea out on paper, use one of the many easy graphic design software programs out there, or else find an example of a webpage that looks how you want your library to look, but don't leave this piece to the whims of someone else. Figure 3.2 shows an example of a library main page.

Finally, you come to the satisfying task of uploading your content into the library. After everything you've done to create this content, whether finagling complex committees or documenting menial tasks, this is the icing on the cake. Before you rush to upload every file, however, take a few more moments to ensure a good learning experience for your users.

Give your videos and written documents clear, learner-centric names. When in doubt, start each file with the phrase "How to." (If you can't accurately name a file *How to do something*, you should reconsider whether it belongs in the library.) If you're using a website or LMS for your library, employ the same design principles you used to create your main page—that is, make each category's page organized and visually appealing. Order the information from most to least relevant. If subcategories are necessary, add them. Figure 3.3 provides an example of a curated category page.

By the end of the curation phase, you have

- Selected a digital platform to act as your library
- Identified learner-centric categories to organize your content
- Created a visually appealing main page
- Uploaded your content into the appropriate categories

TEST THE PRODUCT

You have finally published your library! You can and should take pride in this accomplishment, but the work isn't over. The next chapters will discuss how to train your staff to use the library and how to continually update it based on your district's ever-changing needs.

Before you take on these large-scale efforts, however, consider running Version 1.0 of your library past some users—perhaps a representative sample of new teachers, veteran teachers, and leaders. Share your initial data with them (the needs you're trying to meet). This should give them an idea as to

SAMPLE SCHOOL DISTRICT #123

Here in Sample District, we want you to feel successful and supported. That's why we've created this learning library. You can find immediate answers to your questions about school life, and you can learn to do all kinds of essential tasks using our clear, teacher-centric videos.

LEARN TO USE DISTRICT TECHNOLOGY
- Master the learning management system
- Explore the student information platform
- Apply yourself to apps

FIND ANSWERS FROM HUMAN RESOURCES
- Enroll in direct deposit
- Set up FMLA or another leave of absence
- Learn about retirement plans

SET YOUR CLASSROOM UP FOR SUCCESS
- Use your curriculum kit to its full potential
- Learn about classroom safety and lockdown procedures

GET THE MOST OUT OF EVALUATIONS
- Explore the evaluation framework
- Discover what forms, evidence, and meetings go into your evaluation

Got questions? Reach out to the learning librarian, Mr. Sam Pull, at sampull@sampledistrict.org

Figure 3.2. Sample library main page.

your goals in making the library. Ask them how clean, navigable, and useful this library is. At this point, you're looking for feedback on the library itself:

SAMPLE SCHOOL DISTRICT #123

LEARN TO USE DISTRICT TECHNOLOGY

Master the learning management system
- How to import a template
- How to set up a discussion board
- How to roster your class
- How to export grades to the parent portal
- How to link assessments from other apps
- How to affiliate a rubric to an assignment

Explore the student information platform
- How to view a student profile
- How to access a student's disciplinary history
- How to calculate and enter grades
- How to send a notification to a parent
- How to verify athletic eligibility
- How to view student health and IEP information

FIND ANSWERS FROM HUMAN RESOURCES

Maximize your benefits
- How to apply for FMLA
- How to add dependents to your insurance
- How to set up a retirement plan
- How to set up a health savings account
- How to file a worker's compensation claim

Manage your information
- How to update your employee profile
- How to enroll in direct deposit
- How to report additional education
- How to file a safety or harrassment claim

GET THE MOST OUT OF EVALUATIONS

Learn about the process
- How to find and complete your evaluation forms
- How to prepare for your pre-observation meeting
- How to prepare for your post-observation meeting
- How to provide additional evidence to your evaluator
- How to respond if you receive a low evaluation rating
- How to get extra classroom support

Figure 3.3. Sample library page.

- Can users find what they need easily?
- Does the library draw them into a learning experience?
- Are the directions provided in the videos and written documents clear?
- Is the information contained in the library relevant?

You could even give your test group particular goals ("find the directions for calling home") to see how easily they can navigate the product. As you collect feedback, don't get bogged down in minutia. You're not looking to re-record a video based on someone's nitpicking of your word choices. You *are* interested in feedback on the organization, visual appeal, and overall utility of the library. This is the time to adjust your layout and structure, rather than the tiny details of each system.

The true test of the library will, of course, happen in the fall when the first group of new hires uses it as an onboarding tool. To determine how effective your library is, you'll need to collect data, which means you'll need a plan for measuring your impact. Chapter 5 explores several options for measuring the initial impact of your library. Until then, however, you're simply looking to see if you designed a product that appears to meet the needs you identified in chapter 1.

SUMMARY

- Publishing a system means making it available on-demand to all staff.
- A published library of systems is an invaluable induction tool.
- You should create your library on a digital platform such as your district website, LMS, or social media.
- Curate your content by categorizing and labeling it using learner-centric categories.
- Make a visually appealing main page and category pages.
- Test the product for clarity, relevance, and user-friendliness.

Start the Dialogue

Questions to Start the Work with Your Colleagues

1. Before now, how did we publish our systems, if at all?
2. What groups are we trying to serve with our systems library, and how might this influence our choice of technological platform?
3. What do we want users to experience when they interact with our library? In other words, what should they think, feel, and do?
4. What groups should be represented when we test the product?

Step 4

Train Your Leaders

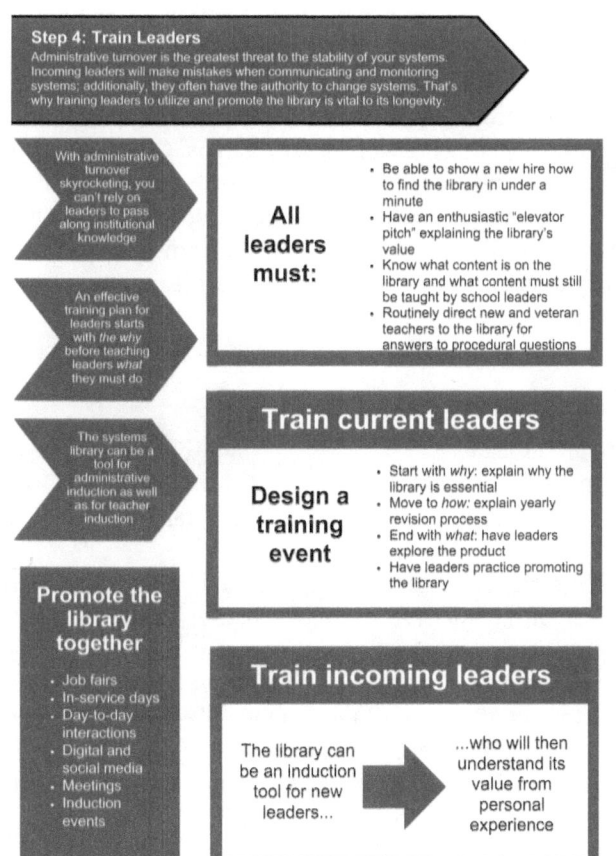

Figure 4.1. Train leaders.

... AND DON'T ASSUME THAT YOUR LEADERS WILL STAY FOREVER

The last three chapters explained how to identify learning needs, create clear systems, and establish a library. It takes a *massive* amount of work to complete those tasks. You don't want all that work to go to waste, so you need to protect your library from the risk of obsolescence. The biggest threat to your work, however, isn't teacher turnover.

It's administrative turnover.

In the 2020s, turnover is just as high among school administrators as it is among teachers. Before the pandemic, one in five principals left their position every year (Harbatkin and Henry 2019). Now, half of all school leaders are considering a career change (National Association of Secondary School Principals 2022). This is one reason why relying on leaders to teach systems to incoming staff is equivalent to building a house on quicksand. Principals spend an average of four years in their role, meaning that new teachers have a 25 percent chance of working with a new principal (Levin and Bradley 2019). Unfortunately, administrator induction is hardly more useful than teacher induction, with incoming leaders left to learn dozens of district procedures via osmosis. That's why they may never even learn tasks that are too teacher specific. They assume that new teachers can just learn these from their peers, perpetuating the cycle of slipshod induction.

To protect your systems library from administrative turnover, you must do three things:

1. Train current leaders
2. Train incoming leaders
3. Work together as a team to promote the library

Each of these steps is essential; skip one and you jeopardize your library. For example, you could have the most intense initial training for current administrators, but if you don't train incoming leaders every year, you're subjecting them to the mercy of tribal knowledge—the very evil you want to eradicate. Then, too, if you don't promote the library to staff, they will never use it, and your team will face the same issues year after year.

One quick note: because new leaders often have the power to change systems, you'll need a plan for updating the library every year. This doesn't have to be onerous; chapter 7 demonstrates how to set up an annual revision process for your library so that its information is always up to date, no matter how many leadership fluctuations you have. Once you've created that revision process, you'll need to communicate it to your leadership team, which is why it appears in the sample training plans in this chapter. For now, though, consider the three initial steps needed to safeguard your library against administrative turnover.

TRAIN CURRENT LEADERS

You need a rigorous, ongoing plan to train your district's leaders—all of them. Every single building administrator, division chair, central office employee, and mentor in the district must be fluent in using the library. Specifically, they must:

- Be able to show a new hire how to find it in under a minute
- Have an enthusiastic "elevator pitch" explaining the library's value
- Know what content is on the library and what content must still be taught by school leaders
- Routinely direct new and veteran teachers to the library for answers to procedural questions

To embed this knowledge in your current administrators, you'll need an immersive, hands-on training event. You can't achieve these outcomes by sending an email or providing a ten-minute update at the next principal meeting. If you want the library to be woven into the fabric of district life, and if you want it to be the invaluable learning tool it can be, you must invest serious time in developing leaders' fluency.

How do you design an immersive learning event out of a mere product? The key is to, as Simon Sinek states, *start with the why* (2009). You're trying to light a fire under your audience so that they eagerly desire the library and feel gratified when you reveal it. You also want to build in serious time for exploring the product and, most crucially, practicing promoting it. Your leaders should walk away from this session with new skills: finding the library, giving an elevator pitch, and more. They must practice these skills in training before taking them into the field.

Table 4.1 is a sample lesson plan you may adapt when training current leaders. It uses Sinek's "golden circle," taking learners first through *the why*, then *the how*, then *the what*, resulting in concrete skill development. It also features several activities you can use to engage your learners and solidify their understanding. There is no perfect time frame for this training, but in general, factor in extra time if your learners are large in number, diverse in job titles, or resistant to change. You want them to have time to discuss data, ask questions, practice skills, hear from experts, and explore the library.

Table 4.1.

Time	Purpose	Activity options
30 min	Examine the *why* Demonstrate why the library is essential and what it will do: • Review turnover numbers • Discuss problems with tribal knowledge (inconsistency of message, frustration for teachers) • Share data revealing time wasted to teaching menial tasks • Explain the vision for library's use	Small group discussions: • Causes of turnover • Failings of tribal knowledge Testimonials: • From mentors or other leaders • From first-year teachers Data analysis: • Turnover data disaggregated by building or school year • Data showing first-year teachers' use of time
20 min	Examine the *how* Explain how the library was created and how it will be updated • Describe the process used for adding stars, nebulae, and black holes • Explain the logic behind the library platform (i.e., website, social media, etc.) • Explain the annual revision process	Testimonials: • From committee members explaining systems creation or revision • From technical team celebrating virtues of library platform Group tour: Facilitator shows main page, describes categories
30 min	Examine the *what* Explore the library and connect to future practice • Demonstrate the value of simple written or recorded systems by showing a sample finished one • Give learners a structured activity through which they explore the library • Apply the library to participants' future practice	Exploration structures: • Scavenger hunt • Bingo card • Open exploration time Application activities: • Role playing/scenarios • Written plan for use in new teacher induction • Plan for mentor–mentee meetings
40 min	Practice promoting the library Develop leaders' skills in selling the library as an invaluable induction tool • Ensure leaders can show a new hire how to find the library in under a minute • Help leaders create and memorize an enthusiastic "elevator pitch," explaining the library's value • Guarantee that leaders know what content is on the library • Verify that leaders will routinely direct new and veteran teachers to the library for answers to procedural questions	Small group activities: • Practice showing teammates how to find library, time each other • Practice elevator pitches with teammates • Role playing/scenarios to practice referring staff to library Full group knowledge check: Quiz or team challenge to recall library content

By the end of this initial training, leaders should know the following: why the library is essential, how the library will function, and what they're expected to do to promote it. They should also feel a sense of eagerness to implement this new, invaluable tool.

TRAIN INCOMING LEADERS

With administrative turnover as high as it is, the success of your library depends on how effectively you train incoming administrators to use and promote it. You can't assume new leaders will hear about the library and learn its value through the grapevine—teacher induction has demonstrated the perils of relying on tribal knowledge. The need to train new administrators, however, is more of a boon than a burden. Here's why.

The Library Can Be an Induction Tool for New Administrators

Yes, teachers are the primary audience. Yes, the library is meant to compile all the systems administrators may or may not know. However, it will undoubtedly include some systems that apply to all employees (applying for parental leave, renewing an education license, following emergency protocol). It also certainly includes systems that administrators will have to monitor, even if they aren't the primary doers (grade calculations, disciplinary procedures, or classroom setup expectations).

Once the library includes a healthy set of teacher-facing systems, the natural next step is to add administrator-specific content. This will increase the library's utility as an onboarding tool for leaders, with familiar benefits: increased confidence, speedier learning, consistent messaging, and more. Some examples of administrator-specific systems include managing budgetary processes, submitting teacher evaluations, and completing hiring paperwork.

You can add administrator-specific content using the methods described in chapters 1–3, and you may even consider adding a category just for leaders to your main page. This gives new administrators a chance to experience the library as a user before evangelizing it to teachers. As your library evolves, it may even feature categories or content differentiated based on job title (principals, coordinators, division chairs, etc.).

You can carve out time during new administrators' first few weeks to walk them through the library content that applies to them. Perhaps they first attend a meeting in which a leader contextualizes the most relevant videos, explaining why they matter to incoming administrators; after this, they watch the videos independently and refer back to them as needed.

Newly hired administrators will probably shed tears of joy when they see the library because of the amount of frustration it saves them; as you know from your own first, second, or third administrative jobs, the first few months in a new gig are less about grandiose leadership theory than about trying to get a hang of new processes and—especially—to answer teachers' questions correctly. Teachers don't care if it's your first week on the job—they'll still ask you to explain the curriculum or demonstrate the learning management system.

With an on-demand library at everyone's fingertips, new administrators don't *have* to know everything; they can point to the library as the definitive learning tool for new staff without feeling guilty. After all, its whole purpose is to provide consistent, guaranteed training, thus eliminating guesswork and patchy messaging from well-meaning but harried leaders.

You can certainly train incoming leaders using the outline depicted in table 4.1, if that structure meets your needs. Table 4.2, however, offers an alternative that assumes future incoming leaders will enter a thriving, functional ecosystem—one in which the library is already a crucial tool—and therefore need to learn what practices already exist in your district to use and promote the library.

New leaders, like veteran ones, should feel ecstatic about the library. You've tapped into their altruism by explaining the benefits the library provides to teachers, but you're also stirring up some self-interest by describing, again and again, how much time the library saves administrators. If leaders see the library as a tool that makes their job easier, they will use it without any reminders from you.

As the base of administrator-facing content grows, so will consistency of practice. Leaderly systems are no different from teacherly ones in that having written or recorded rules generates adherence. In the process of creating content for the library, your district's leadership team may have conversations about improvement that would never have occurred without this chance to formally document policies and practices.

WORK TOGETHER AS A TEAM TO PROMOTE THE LIBRARY

The final phase of leaders' training is to practice the continual promotion of the library, until it becomes automatic. Runners train for marathons by running—first slowly, then quickly; leaders train to promote the library by promoting it—first deliberately, then instinctively.

Table 4.2.

Time	Purpose	Activity Options
30 min	Examine the *why* Demonstrate why the library is essential to district systems: • Explain why it was necessary and how it was constructed • Hear teachers' or leaders' perspective on how the library helps with onboarding and systemic consistency	Small group discussions: Failings of tribal knowledge Testimonials: • From mentors or other leaders • From first-year teachers
20 min	Examine the *how* Explain how the library was created and how it is updated every year • Explain the yearly review and revision process • Explain the logic behind the library platform (i.e., website, social media, etc.)	Small group discussions: Examples of yearly review and revision Testimonials: • From committee members explaining systems creation or revision • From technical team celebrating virtues of library platform Group tour: Facilitator shows main page, describes categories
30 min	Examine the *what* Explore the library and connect to future practice • Demonstrate the value of simple written or recorded systems by having new leaders watch/read a library volume that is highly relevant to them • Give learners a structured activity through which they explore the library • Make a playlist of library content for new leaders to consume after the meeting	Exploration structures: • Scavenger hunt • Bingo card • Open exploration time Application activities: • Role playing/scenarios • Written plan for use in new teacher induction • Plan for mentor–mentee meetings • Create or bookmark playlist for leaders to review

40 min	Practice promoting the library Develop leaders' skills in selling the library as an invaluable induction tool • Ensure leaders can show a new hire how to find the library in under a minute • Help leaders create and memorize an enthusiastic "elevator pitch," explaining the library's value • Guarantee that leaders know what content is on the library • Verify that leaders will routinely direct new and veteran teachers to the library for answers to procedural questions	Small group activities: • Practice showing teammates how to find library, time each other • Practice elevator pitches with teammates • Role playing/scenarios to practice referring staff to library Full group knowledge check: Quiz or team challenge to recall library content

Deliberate promotions start with public-facing products, such as websites and social media. Your district website is a hub for internal stakeholders, yes, but it is also an advertisement to prospective employees. Job-seeking teachers are sure to spend time perusing the site, and you want them to come across the extraordinarily powerful, unique resource you've put together specifically for their benefit. That's why you must find a way to advertise the library on your district website.

If part of the site is already targeted toward potential employees, why not add a banner or sidebar listing the ways in which you support new teachers? You can mention programs like mentoring and coaching, of course, but most districts have those. Very few, however, have a practical, curated, on-demand systems library, so make the most of it.

In a few enthusiastic sentences, explain how the library makes that first year easier for new staff by reducing frustration, increasing confidence, and saving time for what's most important: teaching kids. You may also include a link to the library itself, so potential staff can see it for themselves (this is another reason to make at least part of the library publicly viewable, with no sign-on barriers).

Your district should also intentionally promote the library at job fairs. Leaders representing the district will be proud to display this invaluable resource, which promises a thoroughly supportive first year with the district. They might include a QR code to key features of the library, which potential hires can scan as they wander the fair. School representatives can use their "elevator speech" to explain how conscientiously the district has crafted this resource and how committed it remains to ensuring new teachers' success.

Leaders should also take every opportunity to advertise the library in ordinary interactions with staff. Day in, day out, the library should come up in conversation. To be clear, the library doesn't replace all personal discussion of systems, and leaders should not shoot down teachers' questions simply because the answer is online. However, leaders should bring the library into discussions of systems as a guide, resource, and supplement:

- They might answer a teacher's question about a process, then follow up with an email sharing the library video. *"Glad I could show you around the student information system, Caitlin! Here's the library's full tour in case you wanted more detail!"*
- They should remind their staff of an upcoming event or deadline while providing relevant library videos. *"Hey team, don't forget to enter your grades on Friday. I'm attaching a quick video to this email in case anyone needs a reminder."*
- They can preempt questions by providing videos along with existing informational material. *"Alright, athletic coaches, I printed out the expense reimbursement system from our library for you; it's in your start-of-year folder."*

The goal is to make promoting the library easy and automatic. If the content is helpful and relevant, leaders will want to do this anyway, since it saves them time and energy. Regular promotion of the library will help teachers help themselves, empowering them to find correct answers easily, and it will free leaders to focus on more important instructional goals. Chapter 6 explores further promotional strategies, but your own leadership team should discuss their ideas based on what will work for the district.

SUMMARY

- Administrative turnover is the biggest threat to your systems.
- To make your library impervious to administrative turnover, you must train current leaders, train incoming leaders, and work together as a team to promote the library.
- Your leadership training plans should explore *why* the library is valuable, then explain *how* it works, and finally share *what* it entails.
- Every administrator, mentor, and teacher leader in the district should be able to find the library easily and "sell" it enthusiastically.
- Your leadership team must have a well-developed promotional plan to make the library part of everyday life in your district.

Start the Dialogue

Questions to Start the Work with Your Colleagues

1. What are the most important systems for new administrators to learn? How will we build administrator-facing library content to address this need?
2. What systems are unclear, frustrating, or inconsistently enforced by our veteran administrators? How will we build administrator-facing library content to address this need?
3. When and how will we train current leaders, including administrators, teacher leaders, and mentors?
4. When and how will we train incoming leaders?

Step 5

Onboard New Teachers

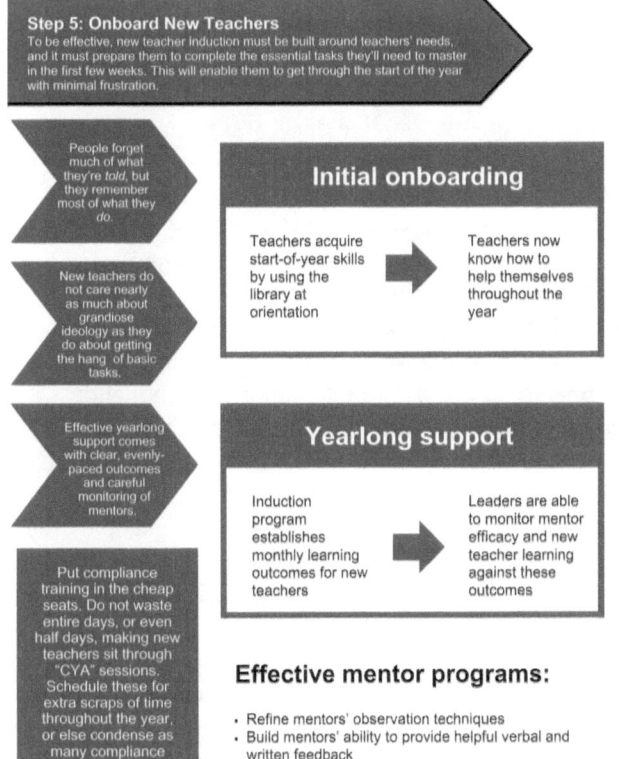

Figure 5.1. Onboard new teachers.

GIVE NEW TEACHERS THE INDUCTION
YOU WISH YOU'D HAD

Publishing a systems library and training leaders to promote it will go a long way toward supporting new teachers. Perfect that support by effectively integrating the library into your new teacher-induction program. Show teachers that you have anticipated and met their needs not only by creating a useful product but by developing an entire onboarding process centered around their priorities.

Their priorities. Imagine how radically different teacher orientation programs would be if they were really, truly aligned to teacher priorities. It's hard to conceptualize, given decades of stale, feckless inductions. Think back to your own first teaching job ... did your employee orientation feature hours of endless lectures, by chance? Can you remember a single thing you "learned" during those? Would your time have been better spent planning for the first week of school?

Plainly put, your orientation, like most, was useless. You didn't care about obtuse HR hypotheticals—you wanted to know what you were teaching. You couldn't focus on the district mission and vision—you wanted to set up your classroom. In other words, you wanted *practical* guidance. Your school's leaders, however, left you to find such guidance in the swamp of tribal knowledge, long after the "orientation" had ended.

And yet, leaders usually forget what it was like to be a new teacher when the time comes to plan onboarding. All too often, they throw together an orientation itinerary at the last minute, lining up a thoughtless jumble of lectures because they believe this is the only way to do things. This is tragically insulting. The event that should inspire teachers instead stultifies them. The opportunity for them to do serious work before students arrive is frittered away on topics that could be covered elsewhere. Worst of all, the message the district sends to its new teachers is this: *We don't care about your priorities or your needs. We're going to do things the way we've always done them while expecting you to be adaptable and innovative.*

A teacher-centered onboarding program must include both an initial orientation and yearlong support. These two components complement each other; the initial orientation focuses on preparing teachers for the first few weeks of school, while the yearlong support sustains them all the way through spring. They also share certain features. Both present information in the order in which new teachers need it, and both involve the library as a learning tool. The impact of both is measured by observing and talking to new teachers.

This chapter helps you plan an onboarding program that honors teachers' priorities and sets them up for success. The systems library will be the critical element; it allows you to wisely allocate your limited time with new teachers, and it acts as a stable backbone to your entire induction process.

DESIGN A PRACTICAL, PURPOSEFUL INITIAL ORIENTATION

Presumably, you have at least some time at the start of each school year to work exclusively with your new hires. If you don't, consider how to adapt the following strategies into whatever meetings or initial communication your leaders do have with incoming staff during August and September.

The first step to planning a teacher-centered initial orientation is to identify *practical* information that will help new hires succeed during the first few weeks of school. The data you collected in chapter 1, which helped you establish your library's needs, can inform your orientation plans—after all, you already spent serious time learning what new teachers believe should be explicitly taught. Some of their requests are undoubtedly in the library already, while others were omitted, either because time was short or because they were better suited to live instruction.

Another helpful mental exercise is to write a "Month 1 I-Can List" list as though you were a first-year teacher, then build your orientation agenda around empowering staff to check everything off their list. It should include everything from small-scale technological setup to curriculum-based instructional planning. Consider the example outlined in table 5.1.

You could differentiate your Month 1 List based on grade level, content area, or even school. You might add to it, if there are specific programmatic expectations (for instance: co-teaching practices, language learning models, or other pedagogical considerations). The goals are the same: to list what a new teacher must know and be able to do within the first few weeks and to turn this list into new teachers' north star as they begin their career with you.

If the list truly does cover the essentials for the majority of new staff, you can confidently promote it as a road map. Ideally, everything on your list would be represented in the systems library as well, allowing teachers to check items off the list using your on-demand material; however, you may decide that some learning outcomes require in-person training during induction, while others may simply not have made it into the library yet.

Your orientation should also include comprehensive instruction on how to use the library, as well as a host of immersive activities requiring new hires to actually use it. The goal is to train teachers to rely on the library as a learning tool, particularly when they need to help themselves.

Not all practical tasks should be taught during orientation; teachers can only process so much new information at once and overloading them will result in

Table 5.1.

Month 1 "I-Can" List for New Teachers

- I can find, comprehend, and articulate my curriculum
    - I have located the standards and pacing guides on our curriculum warehouse
    - I have talked to my teacher leaders about the curriculum and asked questions needed for my lesson planning
    - I have planned instruction aligned to this curriculum
- I can use the technological systems needed for my first month
    - I can navigate our employee access portal, including absence management, payroll, and benefits
    - I can navigate our learning management system for students' e-learning, including posting learning materials, assessing student work, and starting discussion boards
    - I can navigate our student information system, including entering grades, taking attendance, and looking up parent contact information
- Materials
    - I can connect to the printer and copier
    - I have building and classroom keys, as well as a district ID
    - I have received the teaching materials required to start school, including books and classroom supplies
- Policies
    - I can find the teacher evaluation tool, and I can explain the process by which I will be evaluated
    - I have received our collective bargaining agreement, and I understand my contractual expectations
    - I understand our school's policies regarding student discipline and referrals

their forgetting. For example, if you show new teachers how to enter grades in August, they will have forgotten by September. You might not include this direct instruction during orientation time, but you should make sure new teachers know where to find the tutorial, ensuring they can help themselves when they need it. Best of all, the answer is now available on-demand, not stashed in the brain of whatever colleague happens to be passing by.

Like your leader training, your teacher training event must be immersive, active, and centered around *the why*. You cannot simply spend a few minutes explaining where to find the library link and hoping teachers find their way back to it—if that's your grand introduction to the library, you may as well not do it.

Teachers, who are bombarded with information during their first few days forget most of what they *are told*, but they remember much of what they *do*. You must have a carefully planned, skillfully executed training event that builds teacher capacity by having them *do* specific tasks with the library. Moreover, it should flow from and build on the direct instruction you have already provided. You want teachers to leave orientation feeling confident in their "Week 1" tasks and supported for their "Quarter 1" tasks.

Table 5.2 provides a sample agenda you might use to teach staff a few practical tasks, then train them to use the library.

This three-hour schedule may look unusual. It should. Remember, the practice of lecturing new hires for hours on end is ineffective—that's why this agenda features no cautionary sermons from HR, no motivational speeches from hired orators. Those traditions of teacher orientations do not actually prepare new hires to complete the tasks they will need to perform mere days after the orientation ends, and much of their content is forgotten within days.

Hermann Ebbinghaus's seminal, frequently affirmed research found that adults forget 70 percent of recently learned information within twenty-four hours, and subsequent studies have concluded that this number may be reduced only through application and processing activities (Ebbinghaus

Table 5.2.

Time	Purpose	Activity options
10 min	Examine the *why* Demonstrate why the library was created and what it will do for new teachers: • Explain that the district wants new teachers to be fluent in basic systems as quickly as possible • Show how new teachers can get correct information on-demand, thus saving themselves time and frustration	Testimonials: • From mentors or other leaders • From first-year teachers
30 min	Examine the *how* Show new teachers how to use the library • Practice accessing the library from district-issued devices • Explain basic library navigation • If library materials can be saved or downloaded, demonstrate the process	Group tour: Facilitator shows main page, describes categories Q&A: • New teachers have the opportunity to ask anything about the library
140 min	Examine the *what* Explore the library and connect to future practice • Give learners a structured, teacher-centric activity through which they explore the library • Make the library personal by linking it to the Month 1 I-Can List	Exploration activities: • Scavenger hunt • Bingo card • Open exploration Application activities: • Mentor/mentee discussion • New teachers check items off of their Month 1 I-Can List. They are empowered to do so by the library; they may go through their list together with their mentor or another leader, and they may do so in their classroom if appropriate.

1885). A practical onboarding event like this gets teachers into the trenches right away—setting up their technological platforms, exploring their curriculum, and making sure their physical materials are in order. The Colorado Department of Education, for example, specifically calls for induction programs to uphold this structure:

> Rather than front-loading all information for new educators at the beginning of the year, content should be delivered in a thoughtful way throughout the school year and throughout the full induction program. Content should move from simple management tasks to more complex topics such as philosophy, use of data, and strategic approaches as the educator gains experience and professional capacity. (Colorado Department of Education 2023)

After a practical orientation event, teachers can confidently plan for instruction without worrying that they can't log into the employee portal or connect to a printer.

This is not to say that orientation events cannot include *any* discourse about large-scale district philosophy—just that leaders should select only those topics that are truly worth the investment of time. When deciding whether a philosophical—as opposed to practical—topic belongs on the orientation agenda, consider its potential impact on teacher behavior. If you expect teachers to tailor their actions in a specific, significant way following a presentation, you may want to convey the information during orientation.

For example, if your district has strict assessment practices which require teachers to evaluate and report student learning in very particular ways, it's worth spelling out these practices at the start of the year; after all, your new teachers will be required to assess learning correctly from day one. This would be a topic worthy of explanation during the orientation event, as it includes both a *why* (philosophical) and a *how* component. (Naturally, a written document explaining this policy merits a place in the library as well.)

Then, too, consider the topic's weightiness. Highly complex, nuanced topics should wait until later in the year; first, because teachers will be more relaxed, focused, and eager to learn the information, and second, because such topics merit multiple immersive sessions anyway.

Think about a concept like "Teaching students in poverty." What change can you realistically expect to see in new teachers after a single lecture at orientation? No matter how inspiring the speaker, teachers will not instantly transform into poverty-conscious superheroes, abandoning old habits and perfecting new ones simply because they heard a good speech. That's not how adults learn.

Unless you have a specific set of poverty-conscious behaviors that can be taught, practiced, and monitored after orientation, leave weighty topics like this off the agenda; teach them instead over the course of the year through several deep learning events. If successful, your initial orientation should set teachers up to be immediately successful in their daily tasks, reducing their frustration and making them mentally ready to focus on these complex concepts down the road.

If you're considering whether to include a philosophical explanation in your initial orientation, ask yourself these questions:

- What outcome do I want this lecture or direct instruction activity to achieve?
- If you can articulate specific actions teachers must take immediately following the lecture, include it.
- If you cannot articulate specific actions, but instead, hope to get teachers *thinking* or *believing* the right things, consider an alternative method.
- Can this outcome be achieved as the result of a single lecture or direct instruction activity?
- If it can, make sure the lesson plan includes stating your expectations for teachers.
- If it can't, consider ways to instruct new teachers through yearlong support.
- Is this worth cutting into the time new teachers would otherwise have to learn "Week 1" stills, including learning district technology, setting up classrooms, or planning instruction with their mentor?
- If you're not sure, consult school and district leaders, including mentors.

PROVIDE YEARLONG SUPPORT

It's easy to fall short here. The mere presence of a mentor program, a coaching system, and helpful leaders can lull managers into *assuming* they have effective yearlong support. Unfortunately, those assumptions can hide all manner of frustration, confusion, and inconsistency.

Consider, for example, your district's mentor program. How do you *know* that every mentor does the following:

- Teaches his or her protege how to perform necessary tasks, such as entering grades or calling parents?
- Develops his or her protégé's instructional capacity through effective coaching and feedback?
- Covers the full array of skills in the right order?
- Explains both *how* and *why* to uphold district policies, such as the discipline or assessment practices?

- Answers complicated questions correctly?

Those are just topical components of mentoring; this list doesn't even address interpersonal components, such as empathizing, differentiating, and building a relationship with the protege, though these, too, are essential. All too often, however, leaders look *only* at the interpersonal components when selecting mentors, and they assume great things are happening because so-and-so is a great person.

But does this great person work from the same framework as every other mentor in the school? Has district leadership provided her with a pacing guide, allowing her to cover essential topics in a logical order, at a reasonable pace? Does she have the professional learning needed to provide useful feedback, just like all other mentors? How do you *know* she's doing all of this?

The more structure your district provides to the mentor program, the more you can guarantee a consistent experience to new teachers, reducing their chances of drawing the short straw and ending up with an ineffective mentor. Consider this, too: ensuring a high-quality, yearlong experience allows you to confidently pare down the initial onboarding event, leaving some items off that August agenda *for now* in full certainty that they will be taught in other ways down the road. Finally, your systems library just purchased extra time for mentors, who no longer have to teach basic procedures from the ground up . . . make sure this time is used for deep learning.

Ensuring a consistent experience for new teachers starts with setting a framework for leaders—particularly mentors—but you can include administrators, department chairs, or coaches if you have a plan for how they will support new staff. This framework should include specific topics leaders will discuss with or teach proteges, as well as a pacing guide by which they will address each topic. Carol Pelletier Radford recommends mentors follow a month-by-month progression featuring pre-established discussion topics as well as specific learning outcomes (2016).

The goal is to guarantee that all new teachers learn about important topics by set dates; for example, mentors will discuss the district's evaluation process with their mentees in September, administrators will explain the nuances of parent communication in October, and coaches will focus on student feedback during November. An effective pacing guide sequences information logically, introducing each topic in time for teachers to see its immediate relevance, but not overwhelming them. The framework also articulates exact learning outcomes for new teachers. Rather than stop at "discuss evaluations," for example, you might list goals such as:

- By September 30, new teachers will know how to complete the pre- and postobservation forms effectively.

- By October 15, new teachers will understand all indicators of the evaluation tool.
- By November 1, new teachers will understand what evidence they may provide their evaluator to supplement their observation.

Mentors, moreover, must be trained to teach certain *concepts* that are integral to your district's way of life. If you have expectations for equity, relationships, behavior, assessment, feedback, PLCs, social-emotional learning, or any other complex concept that goes beyond a mere task, new teachers will learn these most effectively from their mentors. They should not be expected to change their beliefs and behavior as a result of a single presentation doled out at an in-service day. True change, however, is imminent with the constant guidance of a mentor, a trusted colleague who models the right mind-set and demonstrates the right behavior. Coming from a mentor, the expectations regarding weighty concepts like equity or assessment seem real. They're not fusty abstractions—they're accessible practices.

To ensure a consistent experience for new teachers, you must train mentors to teach these essential concepts. For example, if your district expects teachers to implement restorative justice (a practice that comes with a nuanced conceptual backbone), you cannot simply lecture new teachers once and expect them to apply restorative justice effectively by September.

However, if your mentors are all able to observe their mentees, to provide effective feedback, and to scaffold techniques for an adult learner, you have a much better chance of full implementation. If your district upholds a specific model for coaching—Jim Knight's impact cycle, for example—mentors should be trained in this model before they work with teachers, empowering the mentors to improve their proteges' practice using reliable techniques.

There's also an element of message calibration. Mentors are on the front lines to receive complicated, even outright tricky, questions from new teachers: "Why do we have to do it this way?" "What happens if the outcome isn't what admin promised?" "Can I try an alternative method instead?" Effective mentor training prepares mentors to answer these questions well, both upholding the party line and honoring teachers' right to investigate and deeply understand the system. It also prepares them to work through teachers' reservations and shape their mindsets using constructive coaching conversations.

Mentors' training, therefore, should arm them with the concrete skills they will need to observe, coach, teach, discuss, and guide. Consider integrating these activities when planning your mentor preparation program:

- Mentors refine their observation techniques by watching sample teaching videos and discussing their notes in groups. The facilitator guides

the group conversation, directing mentors' attention toward the key look-fors from the video.
- Mentors improve their written and verbal guidance by creating feedback based on sample teaching videos. The facilitator communicates standards for effective feedback and helps mentors evaluate their work against these standards.
- Mentors develop a plan for teaching complex concepts, such as mastery learning or trauma-informed teaching, to their mentee, complete with discussion questions and suggested reading material. The facilitator focuses this event around the mind-set and practices expected of all educators.
- Mentors practice answering questions their mentee is likely to ask them about district beliefs and policies. The facilitator highlights key talking points and helps mentors to calibrate their answers so as to provide consistent messaging.

The goal here is to improve the reliability of the mentor program, so that most or all mentors provide aligned, coherent support to their proteges. Again, mentors are only human, and you cannot guarantee with ironclad certainty that every mentor will deliver the level of service you want, but training them in the proper skills goes a long way to ensuring the quality of your program.

Cogent, multifaceted, yearlong support, however, extends well beyond the mentor program. It also entails regular dialogue with leaders—administrators, department chairs, lead teachers, coaches, and more. This is a crucial complement to mentorship because of the human element inherent in mentoring. A new teacher may not "click" with his or her mentor, or the mentor may not deliver consistent support, or the mentor may not have the detailed answers needed to answer the new teacher's question, so structures that put new teachers steadily in front of other leaders are essential.

The final element of effective yearlong support is accessible professional learning. Yes, the systems library constitutes bulk of training on procedures, but what about professional development on nonprocedural topics, such as reading strategies, guided play, or inquiry-based learning? Assuming the library does its job—quickly teaching new hires the task-based skills they need, mitigating their frustration, and freeing them to focus on more important topics—there will be a demand for instruction-based professional development.

This is a great problem to have. It means your new hires aren't in survival mode, running around like headless chickens and learning how to do menial tasks. It does also mean that you should have a few options for professional learning that meet the demand. You might consider a badging program, with training open to staff wanting to do a deep dive into particular topics.

CONQUER COMPLIANCE TRAINING AND OTHER NECESSARY EVILS

Perhaps you've had a sinking feeling while reading this chapter. "Yes," you think. "It's all well and good to prioritize practical tasks and prepare teachers for their first few weeks, but don't you know that the state requires us to provide training on a gauntlet of litigious topics, such as sexual harassment? Then, too, our district improvement plan involves weighty concepts like equity, poverty, and social-emotional learning, and we really must provide daylong seminars on these concepts during our orientation. When exactly am I supposed to find time to put new teachers in front of their mentors for long enough to learn a few survival skills?"

State-mandated training is the easy part. Many mandatory topics bear only the flimsiest connection to teachers' daily lives—this is why that lecture on bloodborne pathogens doesn't usually inspire standing ovations. As any human resources expert can attest, states only require this training so schools can cover their assets in case of employee foolishness; given this reality, compliance training should be relegated to the cheap seats, slotted in during whatever scraps of time you have throughout the year.

Maybe you have an in-service day during the winter or spring, long after new teachers have settled in. Maybe your teachers can forego one meeting in order to complete their training module—again, during winter or spring, when they're less panicky and desperate for every minute of collaboration. Maybe, best of all, you can condense the many trainings into a single, easily deliverable format. Although many districts outsource compliance training to hired speakers or online modules, others handmake streamlined slideshows, written descriptions, or videos to get the obligatory message across while respecting teachers' time.

As to those lofty district initiatives, such as equity or restorative justice, start by challenging your assumptions about the relationship between time spent in traditional professional development (PD) and true professional growth. It's no secret that time is the most coveted resource in the world of professional development. When every minute of every day is stretched thin, leaders yearn for a system that funnels teachers into hours of workshops, webinars, train-the-trainer sessions, and more. We assume that if we just had more time for PD, we'd radically transform teaching and learning. We believe that time is the magic ingredient.

We're wrong.

This mentality is, firstly, wildly insulting to teachers. It suggests that they're empty pots in desperate need of the vital water flowing from our fountain of knowledge, and that if we can just hold them under the tap long enough, they'll finally be full, capable educators.

It's also demonstrably incorrect. Time spent in didactic PD is not the primary driver of deep instructional growth. Think of the best teacher in your building. What makes this person so amazing? Is it the exhaustive list of workshops she's attended? Of course not. It's her mind-set. She sees herself as a learner; she takes feedback, tries new strategies, and sharpens her skills each day.

Think, too, about how much institute day time is devoted to PD focused on initiatives, not to mention how many garden-variety workshops your district has run (or purchased, or sent your teachers to). Does all of that time in PD generate an army of perfect—or even compliant—teachers? Of course not. You still have people who break the rules and ignore the admirable practices you've taught them. What does that tell you about the relationship between time spent in PD and improvement in instruction? Teachers benefit most from time spent in *self-selected* PD, not from time spent sitting through workshops chosen for them.

Knowing that time is not necessarily the magic elixir, you can devote your opening days to teacher-centric tasks, confident that you are not sabotaging your district's improvement plan. In other words, prioritize the practical. Those days should go to building foundational skills and systemic knowledge, so teachers have a bedrock on which to develop instructional capacity. No teacher will deliver skills-based, trauma-informed, inquiry-centric, equity-conscious, standards-aligned, assessment-driven instruction if his or her brain is in survival mode.

At the end of the day, what matters is not that you have spent a certain amount of time talking about a topic; what matters is how prepared teachers are after they leave the training room. If they can confidently carry out their day-to-day tasks, they will be ready for your higher-level content when you introduce it via professional learning community meetings, coaching events, mentor discussions and more.

MEASURE EFFICACY

The best way to measure the efficacy of your new teacher induction is to set and track specific goals. Based on what you've read and done so far, these goals should spring readily to mind:

- Reduce the amount of time it takes teachers to learn school and district systems
- Minimize the frustration and confusion of newly hired teachers
- Reduce the amount of time leaders and mentors spend teaching basic tasks
- Increase the amount of time leaders and mentors spend improving instruction
- Reduce or eliminate mistakes staff make when completing district processes

These goals are all measurable if you use the right tools. If you have a set of baseline data—surveys from your initial needs assessment, reports from leaders and mentors, and more—you need only distribute the same surveys and collect the same reports again after implementing the library. The resulting data can tell you whether new teachers' frustration levels are going down, whether mentors spend more or less time teaching basic tasks, and whether staff at large are following district procedures with more or less fidelity.

Naturally, you'll want to complement these numbers with teachers' feedback. Focus groups consisting of new teachers can help provide a more nuanced feedback loop. You'll want to hear from staff who are completely new to the profession—true first-year teachers—to assess their perception of your district's support structure; however, it can also be invaluable to hear from experienced educators who were newly hired by your district, so that you can get a sense of how coherent your programs are to veterans of other districts, those who have seen many ways of communicating and monitoring systems.

Incidentally, if measuring negative features such as "frustration" or "wasted time" bothers you, you can ask new hires to self-report their confidence in district procedures or even to self-report whether they know how to perform specific tasks at regular intervals.

Then, too, working closely with leaders can give you a sense of how useful the library is as a teaching tool. The key here is to find mentors, coaches, and administrators who evangelize the library as much as possible, the ones who truly see the library's potential and who are doing their utmost to increase its use.

This group can assess the library's impact when it has been given its best chance at success. Start by measuring how frequently leaders use the library—how often they link it in emails, refer to it in meetings, and point new staff to it. Then, have leaders reflect on whether and how the library has saved them time, ideally in tandem with quantitative data such as email volume or compliance with procedures.

SUMMARY

- New teacher onboarding programs should prepare teachers to perform tasks required in their first month of school.
- Make time for practical onboarding by cutting out philosophical lectures.
- Train mentors in observation, feedback, and the teaching of complex concepts.
- Create a pacing guide to steer mentors' work with new teachers.
- Deliver compliance training elsewhere throughout the year.
- Measure the efficacy of your onboarding program through a mix of data and personal feedback.

Start the Dialogue

Questions to Start the Work with Your Colleagues

1. Where do we waste time in our initial orientation? What could, realistically, be cut without hurting new teachers' learning?
2. Where can our initial orientation be more practical, hands-on, and useful for teachers' first month in the classroom?
3. How do we currently ensure consistency and quality in our mentor program? How could we better guarantee that all new teachers receive a reliably effective mentor?
4. Where can we deliver compliance training besides new staff orientation? What can be condensed or delivered throughout the year?

Step 6

Promote the Library to Current Staff

Figure 6.1. Promote the library to current staff.

Step 6

BUILD INSTITUTIONAL FLUENCY BY ADVERTISING YOUR PUBLISHED SYSTEMS

The previous two chapters explored how to promote your published systems to leaders and to new staff. Realistically, you could spend an entire year just working with these two groups. After that first year, though, you must focus on promoting the library to veteran staff. This is no less essential than training new hires; in order to make your systems truly turnover proof, every single staff member in a district must regularly use the library.

It should be so ingrained into teachers' daily life that they could not imagine getting through a year without it. They should automatically check the library when they have questions and regularly recommend the library when their colleagues need help. They should treat the library's information as definitive and call out any inconsistencies in messaging among staff—even leadership.

True, this is a lofty goal, but remember why it's worth pursuing: unclear systems infuriate teachers by making them feel incapable of success. If you were a crew member on a ship being tossed around by a thunderstorm, you'd want clear instructions from the captain, and you'd want the first mate and all other crew members to fully understand. Mixed messages and inconsistent compliance would scare and anger you, and they would hinder your ability to survive the storm.

Today's educators must battle a tempest of politics, turnover, and scarcity. The bare minimum they require is a smoothly functioning school, with consistent answers and clear processes. A published library of practical systems acts as a backbone to the district, reducing teachers' frustration and empowering them to succeed.

If you successfully generated buy-in among your leadership team, you'll have a firm foundation on which to build. Leaders will have embedded the library in their daily work with staff, whether that means linking resources into emails or integrating the library into professional development. Now, it's time for a blitzkrieg.

LEVERAGE COMMUNICATION CHANNELS

Schools and districts are awash with communication channels, which offer the most potential for promoting the library. The best communication channel is also the simplest: recurring meetings. Staff meetings, department meetings, PLC meetings, and more—every teacher in every building attends several meetings per month, and these connect leaders with their target audience consistently.

The best strategic move is to capitalize on that consistency by making library promotion a regular, monitored component of meetings. Imagine, for instance, if principals took one minute out of every staff meeting to highlight one video from the library that would be relevant to staff for the coming month:

- "Hey, team, license renewal starts up next month. If you need a refresher on renewing your teaching license, the library has a great video showing you how."
- "Don't forget, final grades must be in the system by noon on Friday. This video shows you how to calculate them according to our policy."
- "I've had a lot of questions about recommending students for Tier 2 intervention, so I'm linking the library's page on this topic into our agenda."

Consistency is key: if you are, for instance, a principal trying to embed the library into your building's culture, not only do you need to promote it at your own meetings, but you need to monitor your department chairs, lead teachers, mentors, and other deputies, ensuring that they are doing likewise. Maybe they follow a preplanned promotional calendar, or maybe they self-report which library features they discussed with their teams each month. If you are determined to make the library part of daily life in your building or district, you need a plan for onstage communication with backstage accountability.

Meetings are also the best vehicle for embedding systems into teachers' daily practice. Imagine a PLC conducting conversations around the example above—the Tier 2 intervention—using the library's video as a compass. Yes, the video focuses on practical steps—probably what forms to complete and where to send them—but having this dependable document in place helps that PLC in several ways:

- It enables the conversation to go deeper. The team no longer has to waste time talking through procedural issues, since the procedure is already laid out for them. They can now talk about how to best support students needing interventions.
- It helps them follow the process correctly. The clear, on-demand information helps teachers do things right the first time, and when brought into a recurring meeting, it becomes immediately real and relevant; this is what sets it apart from the detritus of printed systems sitting unseen in a faraway nook of the district website (or in the deleted folder of staff

inboxes, or in an HR file no one can access, or, worst of all, in people's memory of a long-ago meeting).
- It builds up confidence in the school or district's stability. As you may have seen in your own work experience, a high volume of turnover can shake even veteran employees' confidence and give the impression that the school is a ramshackle free-for-all that repels teachers by the dozen. Visibly clean, stable systems counter this perception.

Meetings, moreover, are the best path by which teachers may work to improve the library. As the library grows, teachers will naturally point out where it falls short—where information has become outdated, where more resources are needed, or where material is unclear. The best response to these constructive criticisms is to bring teachers into the improvement process, and the best venue for that is a team meeting.

Say, for example, the special education department notices that the library's material on student screening is woefully incomplete. Rather than taking on the proverbial "monkey" of fixing the problems single handedly, the library managers should use the special education department's expertise in identifying gaps and fleshing them out with more resources.

This is where the library managers' jobs evolve from content *creators* to content *curators*. Initially, a small group of district leaders banded together to publish some practical systems with the aim of onboarding new staff more efficiently. They did the heavy lifting, from determining exactly what each system entailed all the way to recording each one on video. Now, however, they are helping other staff members contribute to the library's collection, perhaps helping with technical pieces and certainly curating new additions into the final product.

Chapter 7 discusses the role of the library management team in more detail. For now, it's crucial to note that if your staff become interested in the library's quality, accuracy, and success, even to the point that they offer criticism, it's a sign that they see its potential.

Digital and social media also provide abundant communication channels through which to promote the library to staff. If principals send weekly or monthly newsletters or emails to faculty, a simple step they can take is to link relevant library videos into each issue. Like any other habit, the key to making promotion automatic is to track it. As with promoting the library through meetings, promoting it through newsletters, or full-staff emails should be deliberate, with leaders either following a preplanned schedule or else self-reporting which videos they promoted.

The same is true for social media; regular posting has never been easier, with all-in-one scheduling tools allowing managers to simultaneously post to many platforms for months at a time. Your school or district may already have a generous following of staff members on social media, and you can incentivize the others to follow any platforms you plan to use to promote the library.

To make your digital and social media use most effective, make sure your promotions

- Are timely and relevant to a large group of staff. If parent-teacher conferences are coming up, for example, post a video related to that event.
- Focus on what staff may gain from using the library. Remember, this is part of a massive advertising campaign.
- Include links to a specific library video. Don't make users click more than once; make it easy for them to enjoy the product you're promoting.

An educator's day passes by in a swirl of emails, meetings, classes, and hallway conversations. Make the most of every communication—every email, every meeting, every social media post—by promoting the library deliberately and consistently.

ESTABLISH A TRAINING PLAN

Communication, however, is only half the battle. Skills-based training can embed the library as an integral part of daily life for all staff. Just as you trained leaders and new teachers on the *why*, the *how*, and the *what* of the library, you'll find it valuable to do this for all staff.

Perhaps you don't have the time to spare for full-on, multihour training. That's OK. Your full-staff training does not have to take on a traditional, didactic format, nor does it need to be especially immersive. You can blend direct instruction with hands-on practice during staff meetings, spending a few minutes each meeting guiding teachers through basic navigation or challenging them to answer their own questions using the library.

If even that takes too much time away from other activities, create an introductory video showing staff how to use the library. It can be quick, clean, and published everywhere—at the top of meeting agendas, on the main page of the school website, or in your email signature. In any case, the learning objectives for staff are simple. All staff should

- Be able to find the library easily and with no technological hurdles
- Navigate the library well enough to find answers to common questions
- Understand the library to be authoritative

That's it. You're explicitly directing your faculty's attention to the library, and you're setting the clear expectation that they use it regularly. The key is to provide "pressure with support"—in other words, you're sending the message that staff should look to the library first, rather than their neighbor, when seeking answers and directions, while simultaneously, you're supporting their efforts to master your school's systems.

CONSIDER INCENTIVES AND MOTIVATION

As a leader, you know how long it can take to motivate an entire building—let alone an entire district—to adopt new practices, and you know how carefully you must tread when introducing changes to an already overwhelmed staff. That's why you cannot force the systems library on your team. You cannot threaten, coerce, or even respond peevishly to those who don't adopt it. Yes, you want it to become integral to daily life, and you want staff to wholeheartedly embrace its many benefits, but strict mandates aren't the way to accomplish this. Instead, try combining intrinsic and extrinsic motivation.

Your communication and training efforts should generate intrinsic motivation by showing teachers what they stand to gain by using the library. Every time a leader promotes it during a meeting or through an email, he or she should celebrate the time saved and the frustration avoided by simply watching a short, clear video. Teachers' most coveted resource is time to plan and collaborate; a savvy leader will entice teachers to use the library by demonstrating the ways in which it buys even more of this precious asset. Likewise, mentors often feel overwhelmed by the sheer volume of knowledge their mentees must imbibe; smart administrators will present the library as their best teaching tool, the fast lane to skills acquisition and instructional focus.

Simple, daily interactions with staff should also stoke teachers' natural desire for clarity, coherence, and order. When teachers ask procedural questions, everyone—from the principal to the teacher next door—should respond by promoting the library, and the *way* they do it matters. Consider, for example, the new teacher asking how to access students' standardized test scores. A principal might say, "I'm not going to answer that because you can find the information on the district website," but this would be petty and mean spirited.

A better response, and one that generates intrinsic motivation to use the library, would be this: "Great question! You can see those scores when you log onto your employee profile, then click the 'Test data' icon. Want to me to show you real quick? Oh, and I'm also going to show you this cool video on our systems library. It takes you through the details in case I missed something, or in case you ever need a quick refresher. There are also some videos there explaining how to interpret the data and how to recommend students for intervention, which you might want to check out before spring scheduling starts. They're a total lifesaver!"

Extrinsic motivators, such as gamification and public recognition, can also play a role, but be careful. Pandemic-era efforts to boost teachers' morale and acknowledge their ordeals often came across as trite or patronizing, largely because of the attitude they conveyed: "I'm sorry you sacrificed your mental health, your time with family, and your sense of efficacy during covid . . . here's a fruit plate." The mismatch between the effort exerted by teachers and the rewards offered by leadership was what made the latter so infuriating.

When you roll out an extrinsic motivator, therefore, it's important that the rewards match the effort. Small prizes, such as gift cards, lunch parties, or free periods during the day, are appropriate for small efforts, such as promoting the library on social media or via email. Heftier rewards, such as additional payment or power, are appropriate for more significant investment of a teacher's time, such as his or her creation of new content for the library.

Table 6.1 provides examples of how to blend intrinsic and extrinsic motivation.

As the library weaves itself into district life, staff will help promote it without explicit incentives. The clarity and efficiency of published, on-demand systems will make it easier for veterans to help new hires, now that there is no need to explain every process from scratch, nor to direct incoming teachers to a domino chain of people who might know the answer to their questions.

Then, too, veteran teachers will find themselves calibrating their own answers against those provided by the library. Simply knowing that the information is there, in print or on video, will help curb the instinct to guess when in doubt. This will reduce the phenomenon, all too common in schools, in which a teacher could ask the same question of five different people and receive five different answers. The answer is authoritatively present on an easily accessed platform.

When a district has a uniquely excellent program or product, teachers tend to brag about it. If the library acts as intended, with staff finding information as quickly as they could wish, they will be proud to boast about it, most importantly to their new colleagues.

SUMMARY

- To make your systems turnover proof, you must entice current staff to utilize the library in their everyday practice.
- Existing communication channels, such as meetings and social media, will be invaluable to the promotional process.

- Short, on-demand training materials can help staff understand how to use the library quickly and easily.
- Blend intrinsic and extrinsic motivation as you incentivize staff to use the library.

Table 6.1.

Three intrinsic motivation techniques	Three extrinsic motivation techniques
Stoke self interest	Gamify the promotional process
Advertise the library as a massive time-saver for teachers, who no longer have to scramble to find basic information.	*Create a system of rewards for those who help promote the library.*
"With license renewal due next month, I recommend saving yourself frustration, confusion, and worry by watching this two-minute video that shows you the whole process."	"We're pushing out one video per month on social media; the first five people to repost each video will have their duty period covered by an administrator. Then, if you copy me on an email in which you use the library to answer a question, you'll be entered into our monthly raffle to earn gift cards."
Generate team mentality	Reward high-functioning teams
Teachers wish to be part of high-functioning teams; therefore, they should want their colleagues to be skillful and confident.	*Inspire teachers to invest in each other's success by praising and rewarding PLCs who follow systems correctly,*
"You know, you don't have to drain your PLC meeting time taking the new teachers through the curriculum warehouse; there's a tour of it on the library."	"Our course team of the month award goes to the Freshmen Math PLC. Every single teacher on this team set up their learning management system correctly, with the assessments, discussion boards, and sub plans all perfectly laid out. Next month, our focus is parent contact, so make sure to check out our system for parent communication if you want your team to earn that award."
Invite people to be part of the solution	Incentivize participation in the solution
When staff members suggest additional material for the library, invite them into the improvement process.	*Reward staff who help create new content or who participate in the annual review and revision of the library.*
"You're right, we haven't published a video on expense reimbursement, but it's a really important topic. Would you like to take that lead on creating that script, since I know you file expenses often and know the details?"	"If you join our annual review board, we'll pay you for your extra work. You'll also get to shape the way we build and promote the library."

Start the Dialogue

Questions to Start the Work with Your Colleagues

1. Which procedures receive the most questions from our staff, and how can we meet their needs by promoting library resources?
2. What communication channels will we use to promote the library to our veteran staff?
3. How will we train current staff on how to use the library?
4. What intrinsic and extrinsic motivators can help our advertising campaign?

Step 7

Maintain, Expand, and Advertise

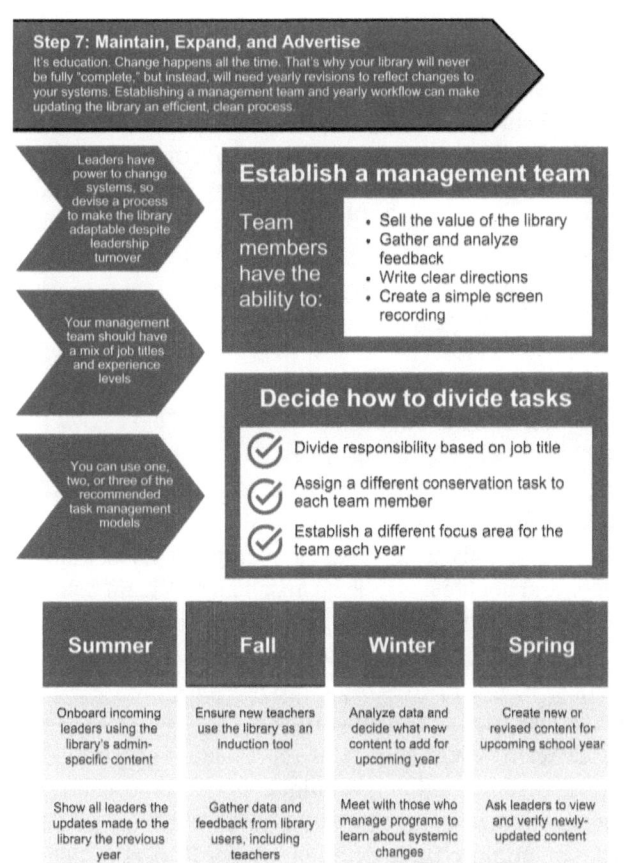

Figure 7.1. Maintain, expand, and advertise.

KEEP YOUR SYSTEMS ALIVE AND OMNIPRESENT

The previous six chapters described the process for prioritizing practical systems, publishing them in an easily accessed format, and promoting them through training and communication. As though that process wasn't rigorous enough, this chapter describes the most indispensable step: keeping the library alive in the face of certain change. It's education . . . change happens. Systems change, laws change, and, inexorably, leadership teams change.

That's why your library will never truly be "complete." This fact should not scare or depress you, but it should motivate you to have a process for working *with* these changes. Your library will not survive if left untouched and unrevised on a shelf, even a virtual one, but it will be invaluable if it keeps up with policy shifts.

Of the many changes that ravage schools, the greatest threat to turnover-proof systems is leadership turnover. When leaders leave, systems fall apart, disappear, or evolve. Your school may have had solid processes at one point, but the most recent superintendent ushered in a host of new rules, rendering the old ones obsolete. Similarly, your district may have had well-constructed, thoroughly published systems in the past, but one person's resignation dismantled the whole apparatus, with no one monitoring the proverbial shop. Don't let that happen to your library. Take a few measures to weatherproof it, ensuring its survival, no matter how many leaders come and go.

ESTABLISH A MANAGEMENT TEAM

The best way to safeguard your library is to establish a management team, not a single manager, but multiple leaders who work together to update and promote the library. This team handles everything from training leaders to revising videos and documents as systems change. A team helps to ensure that one person's resignation doesn't jeopardize the library. Imagine a colleague who managed the library himself for years, only to suddenly quit. What a waste of work it would be to see the product fall into disuse or to stagnate while someone else tried to learn the ropes!

Ideally, your team would consist of representatives from several types of leadership roles—some building administrators, some central office—who would connect with their cohorts to make sure the library was up to date. In a large district, you might want to bring in teacher leaders or department chairs as well. The team should be small enough to fit into a room—after all, you need to have productive discussions and engage each member in important work—but large enough that if two or three people resign each year, the project doesn't fall apart.

For example, a district with twelve schools might create a team of fifteen managers: one from each school, plus three people in the central office whose responsibility it is to keep the published systems updated and in the forefront of everyone's mind. This team might blend administrators, teachers, secretaries, coaches, and even technological staff, so that it can manage a wide variety of systems.

The requirements for participating on the management team include the following:

- Belief in the value of the library
- Ability to gather and analyze staff feedback
- Basic technological skill, including the ability to create a simple screen recording
- Solid writing skills, including the ability to write clear directions
- Ability to accept and adapt to change

To add an additional layer of diversity to this team, consider including a mix of experience levels, from the stolid district veterans to the recently hired graduates. The former group carries deep awareness of how interpersonal mechanics play out in the organization, while the latter brings insight into what new hires want out of their induction process.

SET CLEAR TASKS

Committee management, as discussed, is its own art form. That's why it's imperative to determine how the management team will operate right from the onset. Its members already know *why* they're there, but they need to know *how* they will succeed in making the library resilient to change.

There are several organizational models the management team may embrace:

- *Divide responsibility based on job title.* This model requires and capitalizes on having many professional categories represented on the management team. The teachers on the team take the lead on all library material related to teacher tasks, such as grading and instructional technology. The secretaries on the team manage all library material related to registration, purchase orders, and other clerical functions. Building administrators on the team deal with budgetary processes, evaluation procedures, and disciplinary policies. In other words, this model takes advantage of an intentionally diverse team.

- *Assign a different conservation task to each member.* This model disregards job title, instead prioritizing the technological and interpersonal tasks needed to keep the library alive. In this structure, one team member manages the teacher onboarding process, creating the training plan for new hires, and working with that group to help them use the library effectively. Another team member works with administrators, training them and helping them weave the library into school life. A third handles the technological aspect, creating and editing library videos and uploading them to the online platform. A fourth facilitates regular team meetings, and so on.
- *Have a different focus area each year.* In this model, the entire team works on the same improvement goal each year, with everyone pitching in on an as-needed basis. For example, the team might decide to prioritize teacher tasks during its first year, to prioritize secretarial tasks during its second year, and to prioritize administrative tasks during the third year. Team members all work together to complete necessary work, regardless of their job title, gathering information and creating library materials together as a group.

You can mix and match these models if you have the organizational capacity. For example, you might assign a different conservation task to each member *and* have a different focus each year. That said, clarity is crucial; the team should decide how to divide work, then execute tasks on a clear timeline. As time passes, your management team may adjust its practices based on what works best for the group.

CREATE A PLAN FOR INCORPORATING SYSTEMIC CHANGES EACH YEAR

School policies, practices, and programs change constantly. If you've been in your current district for, say, a decade, it might well be unrecognizable from the time you started. This is a natural effect of administrative turnover. Each group of incoming leaders ushers in new systems or revises existing ones, which is the real reason many districts don't have a streamlined library readily available; leaders either don't stay long enough to see the process through, or else they don't see the point in slaving away over something they fear will be outdated the moment a new superintendent walks in.

That's the most pressing reason to establish a management team, and it's the most pressing reason to have a process by which your library can be updated. If you know change is coming—and you do—you can plan for it.

Below is a sample workflow your library management team might embrace to keep it relevant year after year. As you review this, consider how it might impact your team's makeup and its division of labor; for example, if you choose to incorporate the recommended summer tasks, you must have management team members who can work over summer break. Likewise, you'll need to have team members with organizational capacity to work with new teachers during fall induction. This workflow requires a management team whose members have some positional authority—specifically, authority to determine and deliver training.

- Summer:
  - *Onboard incoming leaders using the library's administrator-specific content.* This sells the value of the library to new administrators, including those who have authority to change systems. Having experienced the library as a learner during their own induction, these leaders will see its benefits and be eager to see the product thrive, even if the content shifts over time.
  - *Train incoming leaders to use and promote the library as a teacher learning tool.* This ensures the long-term success of the library, preventing it from being a one-year-wonder. The library management team must handle the logistics of this training, right down to reserving space and creating a lesson plan.
  - *Show all administrators (novice and veteran) updates to the library.* An annual public service announcement helps to keep the library at the forefront of leaders' minds, and it keeps everyone on the same page regarding changes to systems.
- Fall:
  - *Make sure all incoming teachers use the library as an onboarding tool.* Whoever manages new teacher induction should be on your library management team. That's the only way to ensure the library is a vital learning tool for new teachers. If your district does not have a single person in charge of new teacher induction, gather together those with the most power—perhaps a mix of building leaders, HR staff, and lead mentors—to devise a concrete plan for utilizing the library.
  - *Gather data and other feedback from library users, including teachers and leaders.* The steps you took in chapter 1 to assess teachers' practical needs can be repeated, perhaps on a smaller scale, each year. This will help you identify gaps in the library's content, as well as areas for clarification. You may consider gathering data from new hires as well as veteran teachers, and you may also make deliberate efforts to reach non-teaching groups, such as custodians, secretaries, or bus

drivers—after all, turnover is high among these groups as well, and the library may ultimately include content relevant to them.
- Winter:
  - *Analyze data and decide what new content to add for the upcoming school year.* This helps you to prioritize and organize your work into manageable chunks, so that the library evolves without eclipsing your other work. Consider your team's division of labor as you decide which projects to undertake.
  - *Meet with administrators who manage large programs to learn about systemic changes.* This is why the library management team should consist of representatives from different divisions across the district. If, for instance, your team includes a building administrator, a curriculum coordinator, an HR specialist, a technology manager, and the lead mentor, you'll have connections across the district. You'll know about changes to practices and policies, and you can set up meetings to learn about these and make a plan for updating the library.
- *Spring:*
  - *Create new content for the upcoming school year.* This is where your data analysis and reconnaissance meetings pay off. The library management team responds to teacher needs and systemic changes by creating new written or recorded descriptions of systems. Since you've spread the information-gathering work across the school year, this task should be short and simple—the mere transferring of information into a clean format.
  - *Ask leaders to view and verify newly updated content.* If a system has changed, make sure to run the updated product past the leaders in charge of managing it. This is essential to keeping the library alive. Not only does it ensure accuracy, but it augments leaders' buy-in, showing them that the library management team can be trusted to accurately integrate changes to systems.

If repeated year after year, a well-paced workflow can make the task of keeping the library up to date a fairly painless one. Yes, the management team will change, subject to the same risk of turnover as every other job. Yes, the district's systems will change, bandied about by well-intentioned leaders. The library, however, can reflect these changes as long as those managing it have a system for systems management.

The goal is to bake the published systems into a school's way of life so thoroughly that even turnover among leaders cannot dissolve them. Getting to this point will free leaders to focus on relationships, culture, and instruction.

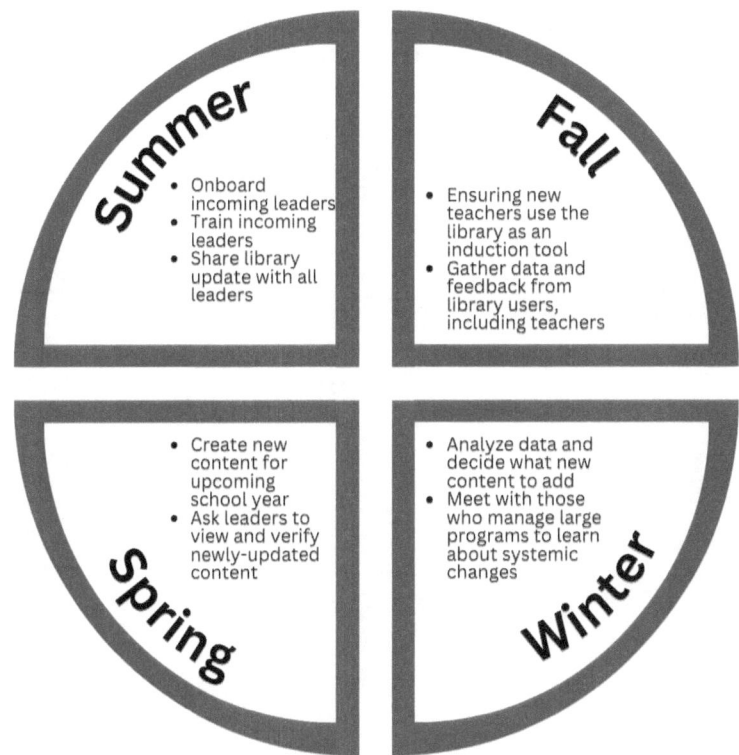

Figure 7.2. Sample annual workflow.

SUMMARY

- Educational programs, policies, and practices change constantly.
- Your library must be able to easily incorporate and reflect these changes.
- A management team with a mix of job categories from across the district can keep the library's content up to date and make it resilient to administrative turnover.
- The management team must have clear tasks and an annual workflow.

Start the Dialogue

Questions to Start the Work with Your Colleagues

1. Given our vision for our systems library, what job groups must be represented in our management team?

2. How will we recruit team members? Should we solicit those natural leaders whom we think may be most useful, or should we advertise the project and see who comes forward?
3. How will we organize our tasks? Which of the models presented in this chapter makes the most sense, given the scope of our immediate work?
4. How will we establish and monitor our annual workflow?

Conclusion

Efficient teacher induction has never been more important than it is today. More than half of current teachers are considering leaving the profession within the next two years (Loewus 2021). Compounding the shortage, enrollment in teacher preparation programs is 70 percent of what it was a decade ago (Saenz-Armstrong 2023). Clearly, every school in the country will continue to face teacher shortages for the foreseeable future.

The average school administrator cannot make the sweeping changes needed to eliminate turnover, such as raising teacher salaries, funding support programs, and revising university curricula; however, school leaders can streamline their induction programs to build new teachers' knowledge and skills quickly and thoroughly.

The best induction tool is one which shockingly few districts have: a systems library. As you have seen, an on-demand compendium of your school or district procedures can combat the frustration and burnout plaguing not only new teachers, but veterans as well. While it may or may not reduce turnover in your district, it can certainly get your new hires up to speed on basic tasks, allowing teachers and leaders alike to focus on instruction, culture, and full-district initiatives.

If your cohorts of first-year teachers seem to grow every year, don't be intimated. Be inspired to meet their needs using the resources under your control. Create onboarding resources showcasing the *practical* systems teachers need to learn quickly. Then, *publish* them in an on-demand format, so staff can access them anytime, anywhere. Finally, *promote* this systems library so that it becomes an authoritative, invaluable resource for all staff, even as it evolves over time.

Bibliography

Carver-Thomas, D. and L. Darling-Hammond. 2017. *Teacher Turnover: Why It Matters and What We Can Do about It.* Palo Alto, CA: Learning Policy Institute.

Clear, James. 2018. *Atomic Habits: An Easy and Proven Way to Build Good Habits & Break Bad Ones.* New York: Penguin Random House LLC.

Colorado Department of Education. 2023. "Designing Effective Induction Programs: A Best Practices Handbook." https://www.cde.state.co.us/educatortalent/inductionhandbook

Ebbinghaus, Hermann. 1885. *Memory: A Contribution to Experimental Psychology.* New York: Teachers College, Columbia University.

Economic Policy Institute. 2019. "More Than Half of Teachers Do Not Feel Supported, and One in Four Has Considered Quitting as a Result." Accessed October 26, 2023. https://www.epi.org/press/more-than-half-of-teachers-do-not-feel-supported-and-one-in-four-has-considered-quitting-as-a-result-challenging-working-environment-contributes-to-the-teacher-shortage/

Fullan, Michael and Joanne Quinn. 2016. *Coherence: The Right Drivers in Action for Schools, Districts, and Systems.* Thousand Oaks, CA: Corwin.

Harbatkin, Erica, and Gary T. Henry. 2019. "The Cascading Effects of Principal Turnover on Students and Schools." Accessed on October 26, 2023. https://www.brookings.edu/articles/the-cascading-effects-of-principal-turnover-on-students-and-schools/

Harmsen, Ruth, Michelle Helms-Lorenz, Ridawn Maulana, and Klaas van Veen. 2019. "The Longitudinal Effect of Induction on New Teachers' Stress." *British Journal of Educational Psychology* 89, no. 2: 259–87. //doi.org/10.1111/bjep.12238.

Kearney, Sean. 2016. "What Happens When Induction Goes Wrong: Case Studies from the Field." *Cogent Education* 3, no. 1. //doi.org/10.1080/2331186X.2016.1160525

Learning Policy Institute. 2017. "What's the Cost of Teacher Turnover?" Accessed October 26, 2023. https://learningpolicyinstitute.org/product/the-cost-of-teacher-turnover

Levin, Stephanie, and Kathryn Bradley. 2019. "Understanding and Addressing Principal Turnover: A Review of the Research." Reston, VA: National Association of Secondary School Principals. https://learningpolicyinstitute.org/product/nassp-understanding-addressing-principal-turnover-review-research-report

Loewus, Liana. 2021. "Why Teachers Leave—Or Don't: A Look at the Numbers." *EdWeek*. https://www.edweek.org/teaching-learning/why-teachers-leave-or-dont-a-look-at-the-numbers/2021/05

National Association of Secondary School Principals. 2022. "NASSP's Survey of America's School Leaders and High School Students." Accessed October 26, 2023. https://survey.nassp.org/2022/#intro

Radford, Carol Pelletier. 2016. *Mentoring in Action: Guiding, Sharing, and Reflecting with Novice Teachers.* Thousand Oaks, CA: Corwin.

Saenz-Armstrong, Patricia. 2023. "Data Brief: How Do Trends in Teacher Preparation Enrollment and Completion Vary by State?" National Council on Teacher Quality. https://www.nctq.org/blog/Data-Brief:-How-do-trends-in-teacher-preparation-enrollment-and-completion-vary-by-state

Sinek, Simon. 2009. *Start with Why: How Great Leaders Inspire Everyone to Take Action.* New York: Penguin Group.

University of Pennsylvania Graduate School of Education. 2018. "The Teacher Workforce is Transforming. Here's What It Means for Schools and Students." Accessed October 26, 2023. https://www.gse.upenn.edu/news/teacher-workforce

About the Author

Elizabeth Dampf has served as an administrator in the Chicagoland area for over a decade. Her articles have been featured in ASCD's publication, *Educational Leadership*, as well as Learning Forward's *The Learning Professional*. She has also appeared on several podcasts, including ASCD Connect, Leaning into Leadership, Anchored in Education, and Principal Liner Notes. She and her husband enjoy food, culture, and travel.

www.ingramcontent.com/pod-product-compliance
Lightning Source LLC
Chambersburg PA
CBHW021215240426
43672CB00026B/319